One Dish Meals

Recipes to make your own gifts

Use these recipes to delight your friends and family. Each recipe includes gift tags for your convenience — just cut them out and personalize!

To decorate jars, cut fabric in 9" diameter circles. Screw down the jar ring to hold fabric in place or hold fabric with a ribbon, raffia, twine, yarn, lace or string (first secure the fabric with a rubber band before tying). Punch a hole into the corner of the tag and use the ribbon, raffia, twine, yarn, lace or string to attach the tag to the jar.

These gifts should keep for up to six months. If the mix contains nuts, it should be used within three months.

Printed in China

Distributed By:

507 Industrial Street
Waverly, IA 50677

ISBN 1-56383-136-8

Pleasing Pasta Soup Mix

1 3/4 C. small shell macaroni
   or other small pasta
3/4 C. dried lentils
3/4 C. dried chopped
   mushrooms
1/2 C. Parmesan cheese
3 1/2 T. dried minced onion
3 1/2 T. chicken bouillon
   granules
1 T. plus 1 tsp. dried parsley
   flakes
1 3/4 tsp. dried oregano
1/8 tsp. garlic powder

Layer the ingredients in the order given into a wide-mouth 1-quart canning jar. Pack each layer in place before adding the next ingredient.

Attach a gift tag with the cooking directions.

Pleasing Pasta Soup

1 jar Pleasing Pasta Soup Mix
1 can chicken, optional
10 1/2 C. water

Place water in a large soup pot and bring to a boil. Add Pleasing Pasta Soup Mix and, if desired, chicken. Reduce heat, cover and simmer for 40 minutes or until lentils are tender, stirring occasionally.

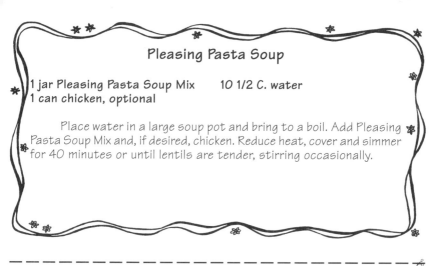

Pleasing Pasta Soup

1 jar Pleasing Pasta Soup Mix   10 1/2 C. water
1 can chicken, optional

Place water in a large soup pot and bring to a boil. Add Pleasing Pasta Soup Mix and, if desired, chicken. Reduce heat, cover and simmer for 40 minutes or until lentils are tender, stirring occasionally.

Pleasing Pasta Soup

1 jar Pleasing Pasta Soup Mix   10 1/2 C. water
1 can chicken, optional

Place water in a large soup pot and bring to a boil. Add Pleasing Pasta Soup Mix and, if desired, chicken. Reduce heat, cover and simmer for 40 minutes or until lentils are tender, stirring occasionally.

Pleasing Pasta Soup

1 jar Pleasing Pasta Soup Mix   10 1/2 C. water
1 can chicken, optional

Place water in a large soup pot and bring to a boil. Add Pleasing Pasta Soup Mix and, if desired, chicken. Reduce heat, cover and simmer for 40 minutes or until lentils are tender, stirring occasionally.

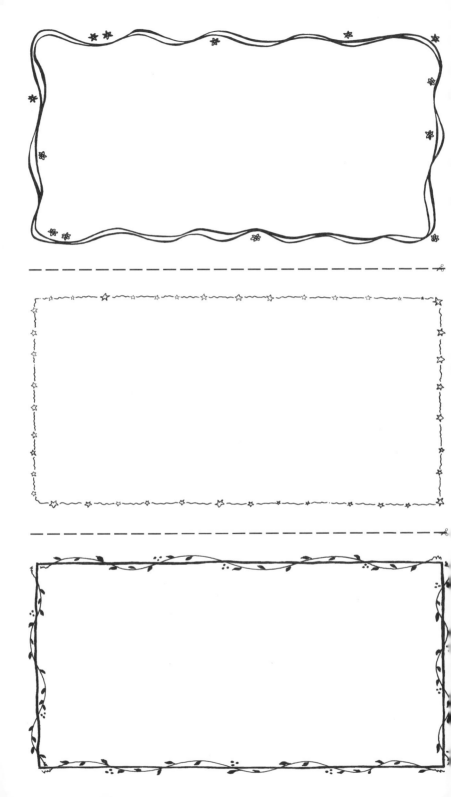

Parsley Pesto Spaghetti Mix

2 1/2 C. spaghetti, broken into
  smaller pieces
1/3 C. dried parsley flakes
1/2 C. blanched almonds,
  chopped
1/4 tsp. plus 1/8 tsp. dried
  minced garlic
1 C. Parmesan cheese

Layer the ingredients in the order given into a wide-mouth 1-quart canning jar. Pack each layer in place before adding the next ingredient.

Attach a gift tag with the cooking directions.

❋ A half-yard of fabric should make eight wide-mouth jar covers. ❋

Parsley Pesto Spaghetti

1 jar Parsley Pesto Spaghetti Mix
1/2 C. butter or margarine,
   melted
2 1/2 C. water
Salt and pepper to taste

In a medium skillet, place Parsley Pesto Spaghetti Mix and water. Over medium to high heat, bring mixture to a boil, stirring often. Reduce heat to medium and simmer until thickened and the noodles are tender, stirring often. Stir in butter. Add salt and pepper to taste.

Parsley Pesto Spaghetti

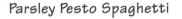

1 jar Parsley Pesto Spaghetti Mix
1/2 C. butter or margarine,
 melted

2 1/2 C. water
Salt and pepper to taste

In a medium skillet, place Parsley Pesto Spaghetti Mix and water. Over medium to high heat, bring mixture to a boil, stirring often. Reduce heat to medium and simmer until thickened and the noodles are tender, stirring often. Stir in butter. Add salt and pepper to taste.

Parsley Pesto Spaghetti

1 jar Parsley Pesto Spaghetti Mix
1/2 C. butter or margarine,
 melted

2 1/2 C. water
Salt and pepper to taste

In a medium skillet, place Parsley Pesto Spaghetti Mix and water. Over medium to high heat, bring mixture to a boil, stirring often. Reduce heat to medium and simmer until thickened and the noodles are tender, stirring often. Stir in butter. Add salt and pepper to taste.

Parsley Pesto Spaghetti

1 jar Parsley Pesto Spaghetti Mix
1/2 C. butter or margarine,
 melted

2 1/2 C. water
Salt and pepper to taste

In a medium skillet, place Parsley Pesto Spaghetti Mix and water. Over medium to high heat, bring mixture to a boil, stirring often. Reduce heat to medium and simmer until thickened and the noodles are tender, stirring often. Stir in butter. Add salt and pepper to taste.

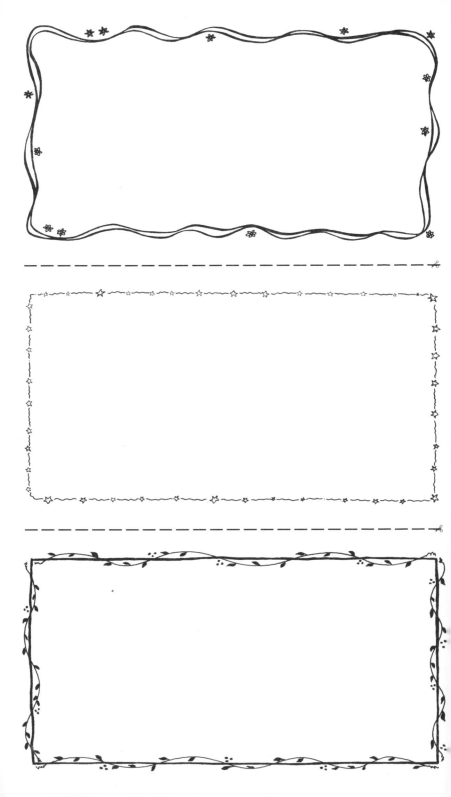

Cheesy Ham & Potato Casserole Mix

2 C. powdered coffee creamer
1/2 C. imitation bacon bits
2 (1.5 oz.) pkgs. Knorr Four
   Cheese Sauce Mix
2 T. dried parsley flakes
1 tsp. salt-free seasoning blend
1 tsp. dried minced onion
1/2 tsp. pepper
2 C. potato flakes

Layer the ingredients in the order given in a wide-mouth 1-quart canning jar. Pack each layer in place before adding the next ingredient.

Attach a gift tag with the cooking directions.

❀ *For a great gift, fill a large skillet or pot with jar mixes, pot holders, kitchen utensils, towels, a cookbook and recipe cards.* ❀

Cheesy Ham & Potato Casserole

1 jar Cheesy Ham & Potato
    Casserole Mix
4 to 5 C. boiling water
2 (5 oz.) cans or 1 1/4 C. ham

Place the Cheesy Ham & Potato Casserole Mix in a large casserole dish. Add the boiling water. Mix well and let stand 5 minutes. Heat ham in microwave and stir in.

Cheesy Ham & Potato Casserole

1 jar Cheesy Ham & Potato
  Casserole Mix

4 to 5 C. boiling water
2 (5 oz.) cans or 1 1/4 C. ham

    Place the Cheesy Ham & Potato Casserole Mix in a large casserole dish. Add the boiling water. Mix well and let stand 5 minutes. Heat ham in microwave and stir in.

Cheesy Ham & Potato Casserole

1 jar Cheesy Ham & Potato
  Casserole Mix

4 to 5 C. boiling water
2 (5 oz.) cans or 1 1/4 C. ham

    Place the Cheesy Ham & Potato Casserole Mix in a large casserole dish. Add the boiling water. Mix well and let stand 5 minutes. Heat ham in microwave and stir in.

Cheesy Ham & Potato Casserole

1 jar Cheesy Ham & Potato
  Casserole Mix

4 to 5 C. boiling water
2 (5 oz.) cans or 1 1/4 C. ham

    Place the Cheesy Ham & Potato Casserole Mix in a large casserole dish. Add the boiling water. Mix well and let stand 5 minutes. Heat ham in microwave and stir in.

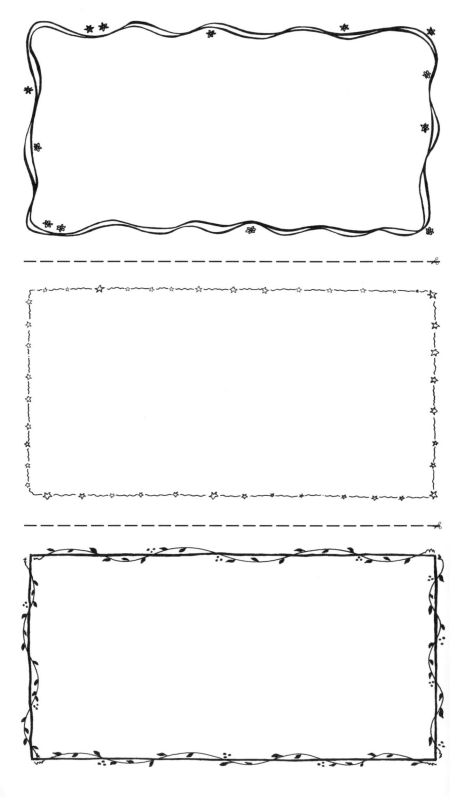

Cheesy Ham & Potato Casserole

1 jar Cheesy Ham & Potato
  Casserole Mix

4 to 5 C. boiling water
2 (5 oz.) cans or 1 1/4 C. ham

Place the Cheesy Ham & Potato Casserole Mix in a large casserole dish. Add the boiling water. Mix well and let stand 5 minutes. Heat ham in microwave and stir in.

Cheesy Ham & Potato Casserole

1 jar Cheesy Ham & Potato
  Casserole Mix

4 to 5 C. boiling water
2 (5 oz.) cans or 1 1/4 C. ham

Place the Cheesy Ham & Potato Casserole Mix in a large casserole dish. Add the boiling water. Mix well and let stand 5 minutes. Heat ham in microwave and stir in.

Cheesy Ham & Potato Casserole

1 jar Cheesy Ham & Potato
  Casserole Mix

4 to 5 C. boiling water
2 (5 oz.) cans or 1 1/4 C. ham

Place the Cheesy Ham & Potato Casserole Mix in a large casserole dish. Add the boiling water. Mix well and let stand 5 minutes. Heat ham in microwave and stir in.

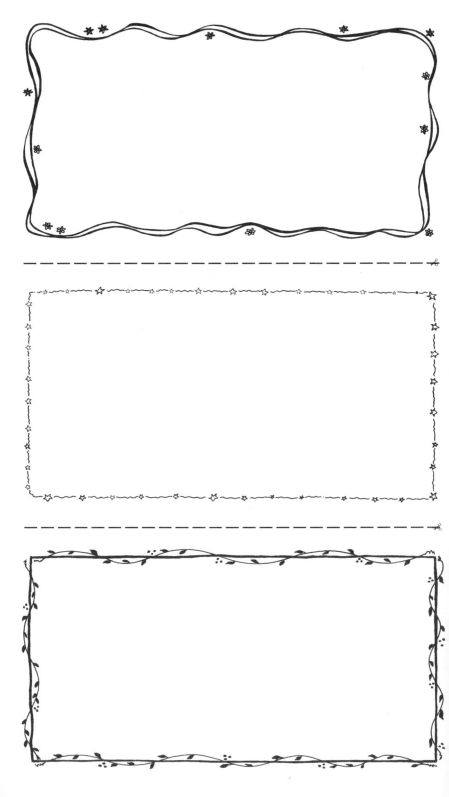

Chili Mix

3 C. dried beans (pink, red or kidney - sorted)

Seasoning Packet:
3 T. chili powder
2 T. dried minced onion
1 T. dried minced garlic
1 tsp. dried oregano
2 tsp. salt
1/2 tsp. cayenne pepper, optional

Layer the dried beans in the order given in a wide-mouth 1-quart canning jar. Mix and place the seasonings in a small plastic bag. Place the packet on top of the beans.

Attach a gift tag with the cooking directions.

❀ *To spice up certain Gifts in a Jar dishes, attach a small bottle of Tabasco sauce to the jars.* ❀

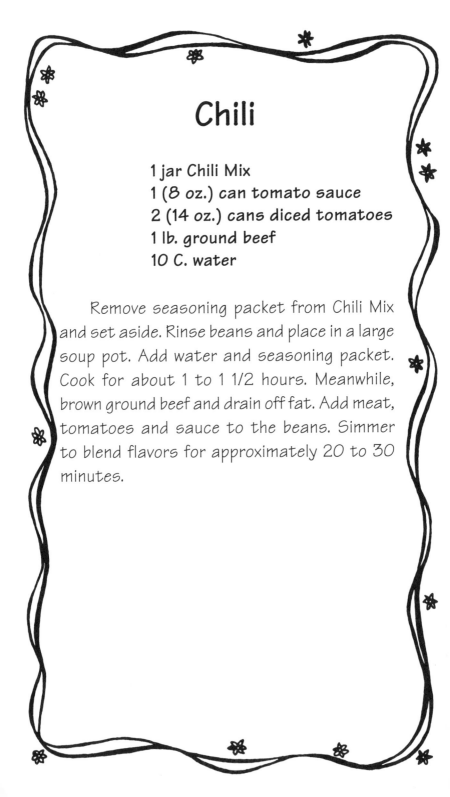

Chili

1 jar Chili Mix
1 (8 oz.) can tomato sauce
2 (14 oz.) cans diced tomatoes
1 lb. ground beef
10 C. water

Remove seasoning packet from Chili Mix and set aside. Rinse beans and place in a large soup pot. Add water and seasoning packet. Cook for about 1 to 1 1/2 hours. Meanwhile, brown ground beef and drain off fat. Add meat, tomatoes and sauce to the beans. Simmer to blend flavors for approximately 20 to 30 minutes.

Chili

1 jar Chili Mix
1 (8 oz.) can tomato sauce
2 (14 oz.) cans diced tomatoes

1 lb. ground beef
10 C. water

Remove seasoning packet from Chili Mix and set aside. Rinse beans and place in a large soup pot. Add water and seasoning packet. Cook for about 1 to 1 1/2 hours. Meanwhile, brown ground beef and drain off fat. Add meat, tomatoes and sauce to the beans. Simmer to blend flavors for approximately 20 to 30 minutes.

Chili

1 jar Chili Mix
1 (8 oz.) can tomato sauce
2 (14 oz.) cans diced tomatoes

1 lb. ground beef
10 C. water

Remove seasoning packet from Chili Mix and set aside. Rinse beans and place in a large soup pot. Add water and seasoning packet. Cook for about 1 to 1 1/2 hours. Meanwhile, brown ground beef and drain off fat. Add meat, tomatoes and sauce to the beans. Simmer to blend flavors for approximately 20 to 30 minutes.

Chili

1 jar Chili Mix
1 (8 oz.) can tomato sauce
2 (14 oz.) cans diced tomatoes

1 lb. ground beef
10 C. water

Remove seasoning packet from Chili Mix and set aside. Rinse beans and place in a large soup pot. Add water and seasoning packet. Cook for about 1 to 1 1/2 hours. Meanwhile, brown ground beef and drain off fat. Add meat, tomatoes and sauce to the beans. Simmer to blend flavors for approximately 20 to 30 minutes.

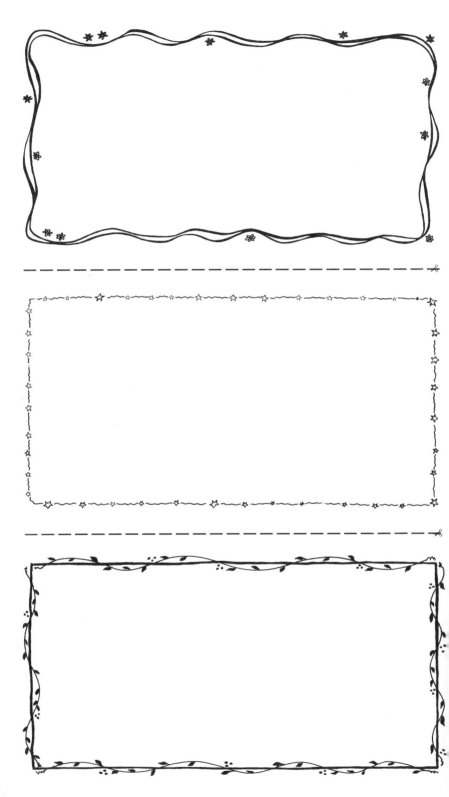

Chili

1 jar Chili Mix
1 (8 oz.) can tomato sauce
2 (14 oz.) cans diced tomatoes

1 lb. ground beef
10 C. water

Remove seasoning packet from Chili Mix and set aside. Rinse beans and place in a large soup pot. Add water and seasoning packet. Cook for about 1 to 1 1/2 hours. Meanwhile, brown ground beef and drain off fat. Add meat, tomatoes and sauce to the beans. Simmer to blend flavors for approximately 20 to 30 minutes.

Chili

1 jar Chili Mix
1 (8 oz.) can tomato sauce
2 (14 oz.) cans diced tomatoes

1 lb. ground beef
10 C. water

Remove seasoning packet from Chili Mix and set aside. Rinse beans and place in a large soup pot. Add water and seasoning packet. Cook for about 1 to 1 1/2 hours. Meanwhile, brown ground beef and drain off fat. Add meat, tomatoes and sauce to the beans. Simmer to blend flavors for approximately 20 to 30 minutes.

Chili

1 jar Chili Mix
1 (8 oz.) can tomato sauce
2 (14 oz.) cans diced tomatoes

1 lb. ground beef
10 C. water

Remove seasoning packet from Chili Mix and set aside. Rinse beans and place in a large soup pot. Add water and seasoning packet. Cook for about 1 to 1 1/2 hours. Meanwhile, brown ground beef and drain off fat. Add meat, tomatoes and sauce to the beans. Simmer to blend flavors for approximately 20 to 30 minutes.

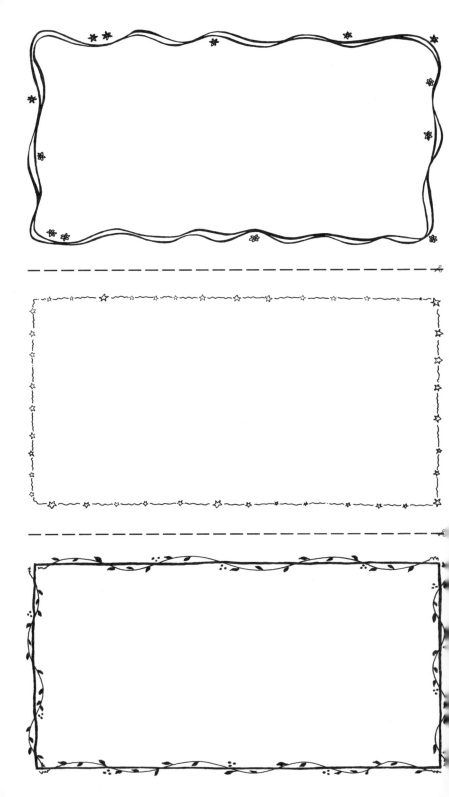

Apple Cinnamon Pancake Mix

3 C. all-purpose flour
4 tsp. cinnamon
2 1/4 T. sugar
2 T. baking powder
1 1/4 tsp. salt
3/4 C. dried apple pieces

Mix all ingredients until well blended and place into a wide-mouth 1-quart canning jar.

Attach a gift tag with the cooking directions.

❀ For a different look, place a small amount of stuffing under a fabric cover before attaching to "puff" the top. ❀

Apple Cinnamon Pancakes

To make 5 servings:
1 1/3 C. Apple Cinnamon Pancake
  Mix
3/4 C. milk
1 egg
2 T. vegetable oil

In a medium bowl, combine milk, egg and vegetable oil. Whisk in Apple Cinnamon Pancake Mix until moistened but still lumpy. Heat a lightly oiled griddle or frying pan over medium high heat. Pour batter, 1/4 cup at a time, onto the prepared griddle. Cook on both sides until golden brown, flipping when the surface begins to bubble.

Apple Cinnamon Pancakes

To make 5 servings:

1 1/3 C. Apple Cinnamon
   Pancake Mix
3/4 C. milk

1 egg
2 T. vegetable oil

     In a medium bowl, combine milk, egg and vegetable oil. Whisk in Apple Cinnamon Pancake Mix until moistened but still lumpy. Heat a lightly oiled griddle or frying pan over medium high heat. Pour batter, 1/4 cup at a time, onto the prepared griddle. Cook on both sides until golden brown, flipping when the surface begins to bubble.

Apple Cinnamon Pancakes

To make 5 servings:

1 1/3 C. Apple Cinnamon
   Pancake Mix
3/4 C. milk

1 egg
2 T. vegetable oil

     In a medium bowl, combine milk, egg and vegetable oil. Whisk in Apple Cinnamon Pancake Mix until moistened but still lumpy. Heat a lightly oiled griddle or frying pan over medium high heat. Pour batter, 1/4 cup at a time, onto the prepared griddle. Cook on both sides until golden brown, flipping when the surface begins to bubble.

Apple Cinnamon Pancakes

To make 5 servings:

1 1/3 C. Apple Cinnamon
   Pancake Mix
3/4 C. milk

1 egg
2 T. vegetable oil

     In a medium bowl, combine milk, egg and vegetable oil. Whisk in Apple Cinnamon Pancake Mix until moistened but still lumpy. Heat a lightly oiled griddle or frying pan over medium high heat. Pour batter, 1/4 cup at a time, onto the prepared griddle. Cook on both sides until golden brown, flipping when the surface begins to bubble.

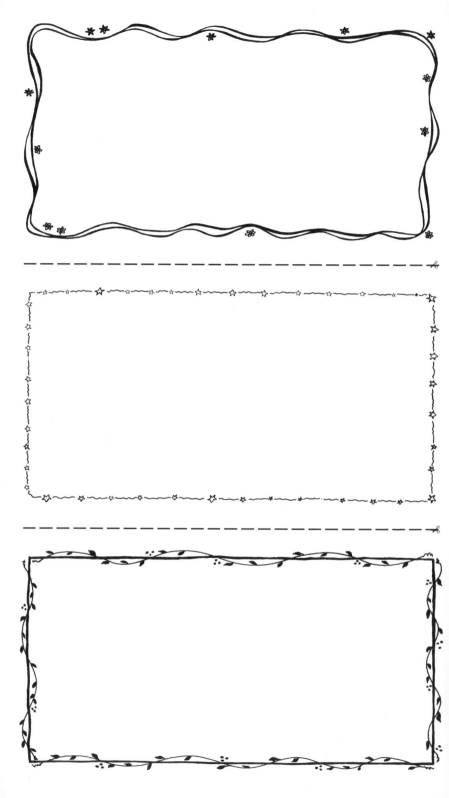

Apple Cinnamon Pancakes

To make 5 servings:

1 1/3 C. Apple Cinnamon
   Pancake Mix
3/4 C. milk

1 egg
2 T. vegetable oil

In a medium bowl, combine milk, egg and vegetable oil. Whisk in Apple Cinnamon Pancake Mix until moistened but still lumpy. Heat a lightly oiled griddle or frying pan over medium high heat. Pour batter, 1/4 cup at a time, onto the prepared griddle. Cook on both sides until golden brown, flipping when the surface begins to bubble.

Apple Cinnamon Pancakes

To make 5 servings:

1 1/3 C. Apple Cinnamon
   Pancake Mix
3/4 C. milk

1 egg
2 T. vegetable oil

In a medium bowl, combine milk, egg and vegetable oil. Whisk in Apple Cinnamon Pancake Mix until moistened but still lumpy. Heat a lightly oiled griddle or frying pan over medium high heat. Pour batter, 1/4 cup at a time, onto the prepared griddle. Cook on both sides until golden brown, flipping when the surface begins to bubble.

Apple Cinnamon Pancakes

To make 5 servings:

1 1/3 C. Apple Cinnamon
   Pancake Mix
3/4 C. milk

1 egg
2 T. vegetable oil

In a medium bowl, combine milk, egg and vegetable oil. Whisk in Apple Cinnamon Pancake Mix until moistened but still lumpy. Heat a lightly oiled griddle or frying pan over medium high heat. Pour batter, 1/4 cup at a time, onto the prepared griddle. Cook on both sides until golden brown, flipping when the surface begins to bubble.

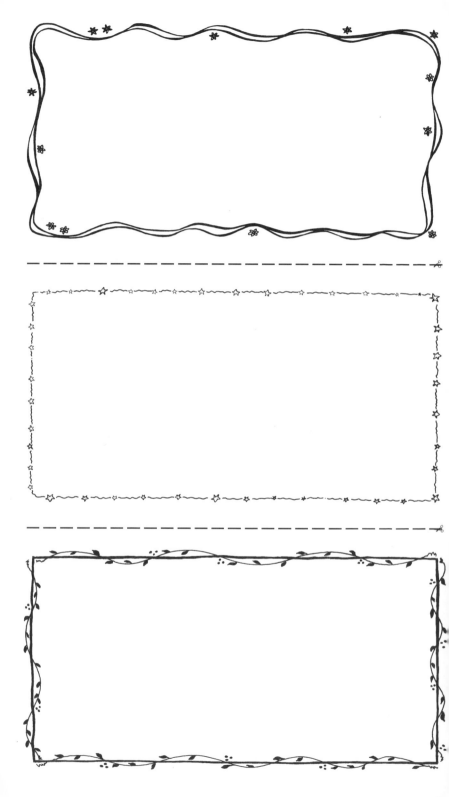

Jambalaya Mix

3 C. long-grain white rice
2 1/2 T. dried minced onion
2 1/2 T. green bell pepper flakes
2 1/2 T. dried parsley flakes
2 bay leaves (place down the
   side of the jar)
2 T. plus 1 tsp. beef bouillon
   granules
1 1/4 tsp. garlic powder
1 1/4 tsp. pepper
1 1/4 tsp. dried thyme
3/4 to 1 1/4 tsp. crushed red
   pepper

Layer the ingredients in the order given into a wide-mouth 1-quart canning jar. Pack each layer in place before adding the next ingredient.

Attach a gift tag with the cooking directions.

❀ For an out of the ordinary gift, place jar mixes in a mixing bowl along with kitchen utensils, cookbooks, recipe cards, towels and pot holders. ❀

Jambalaya

Makes 6 servings

1 jar Jambalaya Mix
7 1/2 C. water
1 (20 oz.) can tomato sauce
1 1/4 C. cooked ham or smoked
   sausage
1 1/4 C. cooked shrimp

In a large skillet, combine Jambalaya Mix, water and tomato sauce and bring to a boil. Reduce heat to simmer; add ham or sausage and cook 20 more minutes. Add shrimp and cook 5 minutes more. Remove and discard bay leaves.

Jambalaya

Makes 6 servings

1 jar Jambalaya Mix	1 1/4 C. cooked ham or smoked
7 1/2 C. water	sausage
1 (20 oz.) can tomato sauce	1 1/4 C. cooked shrimp

In a large skillet, combine Jambalaya Mix, water and tomato sauce and bring to a boil. Reduce heat to simmer; add ham or sausage and cook 20 more minutes. Add shrimp and cook 5 minutes more. Remove and discard bay leaves.

Jambalaya

Makes 6 servings

1 jar Jambalaya Mix	1 1/4 C. cooked ham or smoked
7 1/2 C. water	sausage
1 (20 oz.) can tomato sauce	1 1/4 C. cooked shrimp

In a large skillet, combine Jambalaya Mix, water and tomato sauce and bring to a boil. Reduce heat to simmer; add ham or sausage and cook 20 more minutes. Add shrimp and cook 5 minutes more. Remove and discard bay leaves.

Jambalaya

Makes 6 servings

1 jar Jambalaya Mix	1 1/4 C. cooked ham or smoked
7 1/2 C. water	sausage
1 (20 oz.) can tomato sauce	1 1/4 C. cooked shrimp

In a large skillet, combine Jambalaya Mix, water and tomato sauce and bring to a boil. Reduce heat to simmer; add ham or sausage and cook 20 more minutes. Add shrimp and cook 5 minutes more. Remove and discard bay leaves.

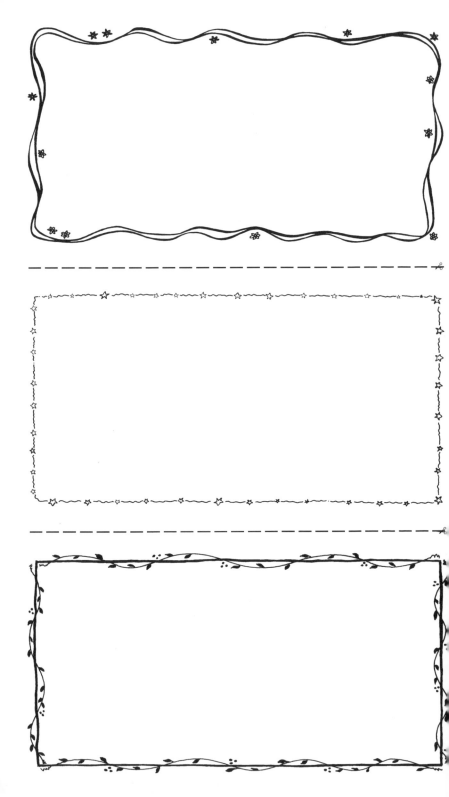

Jambalaya
Makes 6 servings

1 jar Jambalaya Mix
7 1/2 C. water
1 (20 oz.) can tomato sauce

1 1/4 C. cooked ham or smoked
    sausage
1 1/4 C. cooked shrimp

In a large skillet, combine Jambalaya Mix, water and tomato sauce and bring to a boil. Reduce heat to simmer; add ham or sausage and cook 20 more minutes. Add shrimp and cook 5 minutes more. Remove and discard bay leaves.

Jambalaya
Makes 6 servings

1 jar Jambalaya Mix
7 1/2 C. water
1 (20 oz.) can tomato sauce

1 1/4 C. cooked ham or smoked
    sausage
1 1/4 C. cooked shrimp

In a large skillet, combine Jambalaya Mix, water and tomato sauce and bring to a boil. Reduce heat to simmer; add ham or sausage and cook 20 more minutes. Add shrimp and cook 5 minutes more. Remove and discard bay leaves.

Jambalaya
Makes 6 servings

1 jar Jambalaya Mix
7 1/2 C. water
1 (20 oz.) can tomato sauce

1 1/4 C. cooked ham or smoked
    sausage
1 1/4 C. cooked shrimp

In a large skillet, combine Jambalaya Mix, water and tomato sauce and bring to a boil. Reduce heat to simmer; add ham or sausage and cook 20 more minutes. Add shrimp and cook 5 minutes more. Remove and discard bay leaves.

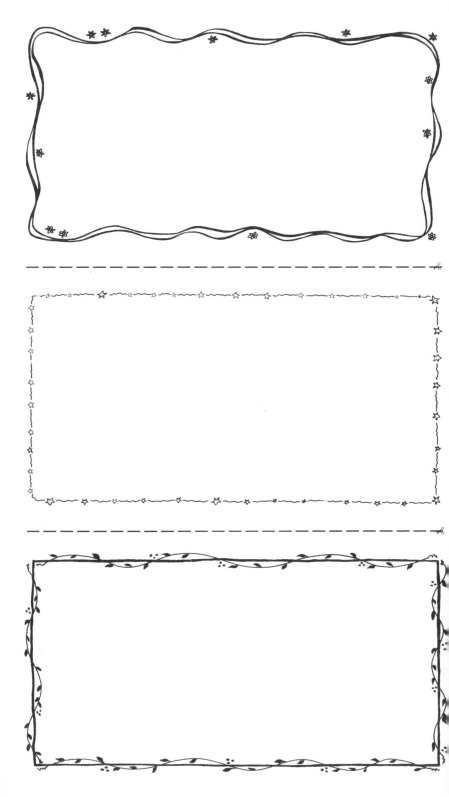

Pasta Fagioli Mix

3/4 C. dried great northern beans
3/4 C. dried pinto beans
3/4 C. dried red beans
1 bay leaf (place down the side of the jar)

Seasoning Packet:

1/4 C. dried minced onion
2 tsp. dried minced garlic
1 tsp. dried oregano
1 tsp. dried basil
1/2 tsp. dried celery flakes
1/2 tsp. dried rosemary
3/4 tsp. salt
1/8 tsp. crushed red pepper

1 1/4 C. small pasta shells in a baggie

Layer the ingredients in the order given into a wide-mouth 1-quart canning jar. Mix and place the seasonings in a small plastic bag. Place the packet on top of the beans. Place pasta on top of seasoning packet.

Attach a gift tag with the cooking directions.

Pasta Fagioli

1 jar Pasta Fagioli Mix
2 T. olive oil
1 carrot, chopped
1 stalk celery, chopped
1 C. chopped ham
2 (28 oz.) cans Italian plum
   tomatoes, chopped
4 C. chicken stock or water
Parmesan cheese, optional

Remove bags from Pasta Fagioli Mix. Wash beans and set aside. In a large soup pot, sauté carrot, celery and ham in olive oil. Add tomatoes, chicken stock or water, beans and seasoning mix. Bring to a boil. Cover partially, reduce heat and simmer 2 to 3 hours or until beans are tender. Pasta may be added now. Cook 5 to 7 minutes or until pasta is al dente. Remove and discard bay leaf. Garnish with Parmesan cheese if desired.

Pasta Fagioli

1 jar Pasta Fagioli Mix
2 T. olive oil
1 carrot, chopped
1 stalk celery, chopped
1 C. chopped ham

2 (28 oz.) cans Italian plum
  tomatoes, chopped
4 C. chicken stock or water
Parmesan cheese, optional

Remove bags from Pasta Fagioli Mix. Wash beans and set aside. In a large soup pot, sauté carrot, celery and ham in olive oil. Add tomatoes, chicken stock or water, beans and seasoning mix. Bring to a boil. Cover partially, reduce heat and simmer 2 to 3 hours or until beans are tender. Pasta may be added now. Cook 5 to 7 minutes or until pasta is al dente. Remove and discard bay leaf. Garnish with Parmesan cheese if desired.

Pasta Fagioli

1 jar Pasta Fagioli Mix
2 T. olive oil
1 carrot, chopped
1 stalk celery, chopped
1 C. chopped ham

2 (28 oz.) cans Italian plum
  tomatoes, chopped
4 C. chicken stock or water
Parmesan cheese, optional

Remove bags from Pasta Fagioli Mix. Wash beans and set aside. In a large soup pot, sauté carrot, celery and ham in olive oil. Add tomatoes, chicken stock or water, beans and seasoning mix. Bring to a boil. Cover partially, reduce heat and simmer 2 to 3 hours or until beans are tender. Pasta may be added now. Cook 5 to 7 minutes or until pasta is al dente. Remove and discard bay leaf. Garnish with Parmesan cheese if desired.

Pasta Fagioli

1 jar Pasta Fagioli Mix
2 T. olive oil
1 carrot, chopped
1 stalk celery, chopped
1 C. chopped ham

2 (28 oz.) cans Italian plum
  tomatoes, chopped
4 C. chicken stock or water
Parmesan cheese, optional

Remove bags from Pasta Fagioli Mix. Wash beans and set aside. In a large soup pot, sauté carrot, celery and ham in olive oil. Add tomatoes, chicken stock or water, beans and seasoning mix. Bring to a boil. Cover partially, reduce heat and simmer 2 to 3 hours or until beans are tender. Pasta may be added now. Cook 5 to 7 minutes or until pasta is al dente. Remove and discard bay leaf. Garnish with Parmesan cheese if desired.

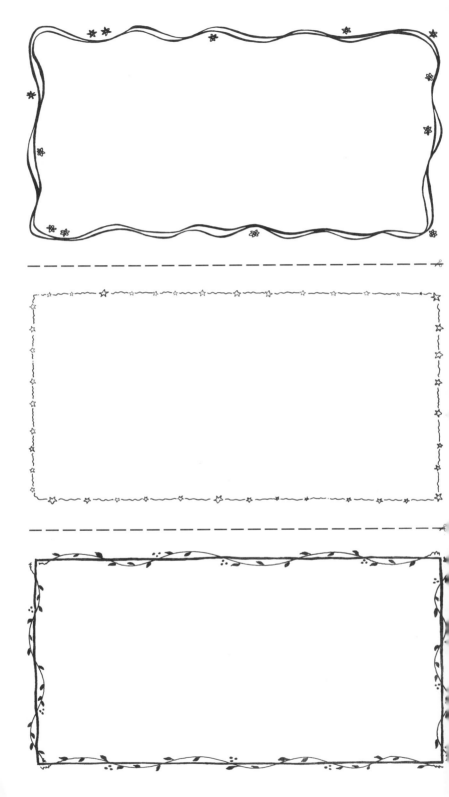

Pasta Fagioli

1 jar Pasta Fagioli Mix
2 T. olive oil
1 carrot, chopped
1 stalk celery, chopped
1 C. chopped ham

2 (28 oz.) cans Italian plum
   tomatoes, chopped
4 C. chicken stock or water
Parmesan cheese, optional

Remove bags from Pasta Fagioli Mix. Wash beans and set aside. In a large soup pot, sauté carrot, celery and ham in olive oil. Add tomatoes, chicken stock or water, beans and seasoning mix. Bring to a boil. Cover partially, reduce heat and simmer 2 to 3 hours or until beans are tender. Pasta may be added now. Cook 5 to 7 minutes or until pasta is al dente. Remove and discard bay leaf. Garnish with Parmesan cheese if desired.

Pasta Fagioli

1 jar Pasta Fagioli Mix
2 T. olive oil
1 carrot, chopped
1 stalk celery, chopped
1 C. chopped ham

2 (28 oz.) cans Italian plum
   tomatoes, chopped
4 C. chicken stock or water
Parmesan cheese, optional

Remove bags from Pasta Fagioli Mix. Wash beans and set aside. In a large soup pot, sauté carrot, celery and ham in olive oil. Add tomatoes, chicken stock or water, beans and seasoning mix. Bring to a boil. Cover partially, reduce heat and simmer 2 to 3 hours or until beans are tender. Pasta may be added now. Cook 5 to 7 minutes or until pasta is al dente. Remove and discard bay leaf. Garnish with Parmesan cheese if desired.

Pasta Fagioli

1 jar Pasta Fagioli Mix
2 T. olive oil
1 carrot, chopped
1 stalk celery, chopped
1 C. chopped ham

2 (28 oz.) cans Italian plum
   tomatoes, chopped
4 C. chicken stock or water
Parmesan cheese, optional

Remove bags from Pasta Fagioli Mix. Wash beans and set aside. In a large soup pot, sauté carrot, celery and ham in olive oil. Add tomatoes, chicken stock or water, beans and seasoning mix. Bring to a boil. Cover partially, reduce heat and simmer 2 to 3 hours or until beans are tender. Pasta may be added now. Cook 5 to 7 minutes or until pasta is al dente. Remove and discard bay leaf. Garnish with Parmesan cheese if desired.

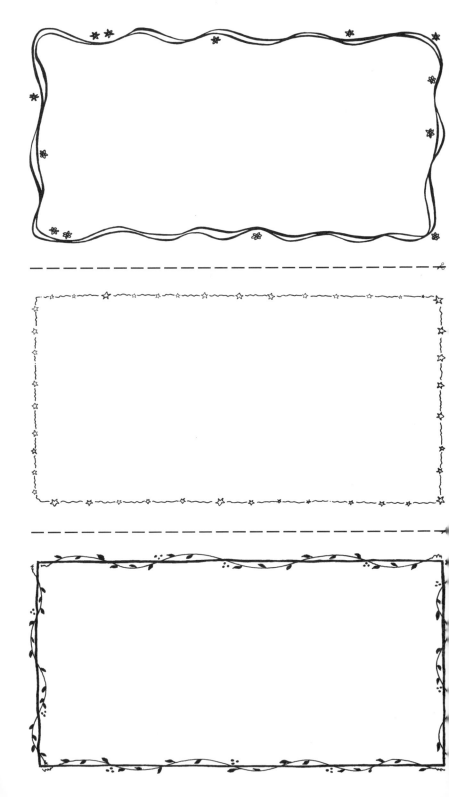

Chili Tomato Mac Mix

1/2 C. plus 2 T. instant dry milk
1/3 C. cornstarch
1 T. plus 1 tsp. chicken or beef
   bouillon granules
2 tsp. dried minced onion
1/4 tsp. plus 1/8 tsp. dried
   basil
1/4 tsp. plus 1/8 tsp. dried
   thyme
1/4 tsp. plus 1/8 tsp. pepper
2 tsp. dried parsley flakes
1 tsp. garlic powder
2 T. chili powder
3 C. macaroni

Layer the ingredients in the order given into a wide-mouth 1-quart canning jar. Pack each layer in place before adding the next ingredient.

Attach a gift tag with the cooking directions.

Chili Tomato Mac

Makes 8 to 10 servings

1 jar Chili Tomato Mac Mix
1 1/2 lbs. ground beef
3 (15 oz.) cans chopped
   tomatoes
2 C. water

In a large skillet, brown ground beef and drain off the fat. Add Chili Tomato Mac Mix, chopped tomatoes and water. Simmer covered 20 minutes or until macaroni is tender, stirring often.

Chili Tomato Mac
Makes 8 to 10 servings

1 jar Chili Tomato Mac Mix   3 (15 oz.) cans chopped tomatoes
1 1/2 lbs. ground beef   2 C. water

In a large skillet, brown ground beef and drain off the fat. Add Chili Tomato Mac Mix, chopped tomatoes and water. Simmer covered 20 minutes or until macaroni is tender, stirring often.

Chili Tomato Mac
Makes 8 to 10 servings

1 jar Chili Tomato Mac Mix   3 (15 oz.) cans chopped tomatoes
1 1/2 lbs. ground beef   2 C. water

In a large skillet, brown ground beef and drain off the fat. Add Chili Tomato Mac Mix, chopped tomatoes and water. Simmer covered 20 minutes or until macaroni is tender, stirring often.

Chili Tomato Mac
Makes 8 to 10 servings

1 jar Chili Tomato Mac Mix   3 (15 oz.) cans chopped tomatoes
1 1/2 lbs. ground beef   2 C. water

In a large skillet, brown ground beef and drain off the fat. Add Chili Tomato Mac Mix, chopped tomatoes and water. Simmer covered 20 minutes or until macaroni is tender, stirring often.

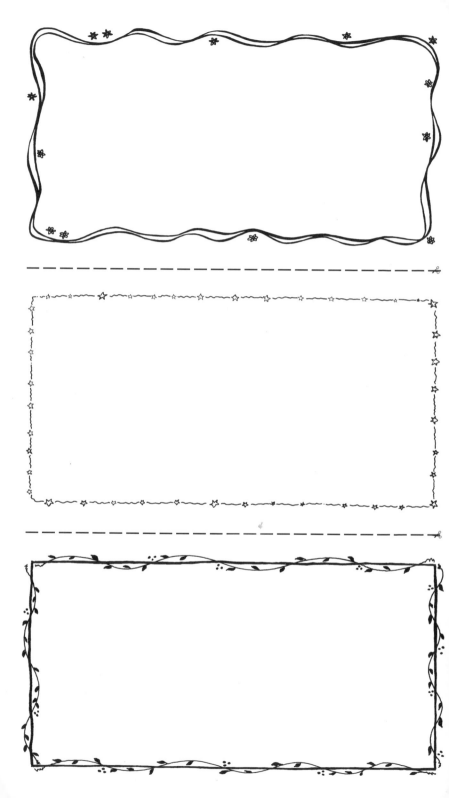

Chili Tomato Mac
Makes 8 to 10 servings

1 jar Chili Tomato Mac Mix
1 1/2 lbs. ground beef

3 (15 oz.) cans chopped tomatoes
2 C. water

In a large skillet, brown ground beef and drain off the fat. Add Chili Tomato Mac Mix, chopped tomatoes and water. Simmer covered 20 minutes or until macaroni is tender, stirring often.

Chili Tomato Mac
Makes 8 to 10 servings

1 jar Chili Tomato Mac Mix
1 1/2 lbs. ground beef

3 (15 oz.) cans chopped tomatoes
2 C. water

In a large skillet, brown ground beef and drain off the fat. Add Chili Tomato Mac Mix, chopped tomatoes and water. Simmer covered 20 minutes or until macaroni is tender, stirring often.

Chili Tomato Mac
Makes 8 to 10 servings

1 jar Chili Tomato Mac Mix
1 1/2 lbs. ground beef

3 (15 oz.) cans chopped tomatoes
2 C. water

In a large skillet, brown ground beef and drain off the fat. Add Chili Tomato Mac Mix, chopped tomatoes and water. Simmer covered 20 minutes or until macaroni is tender, stirring often.

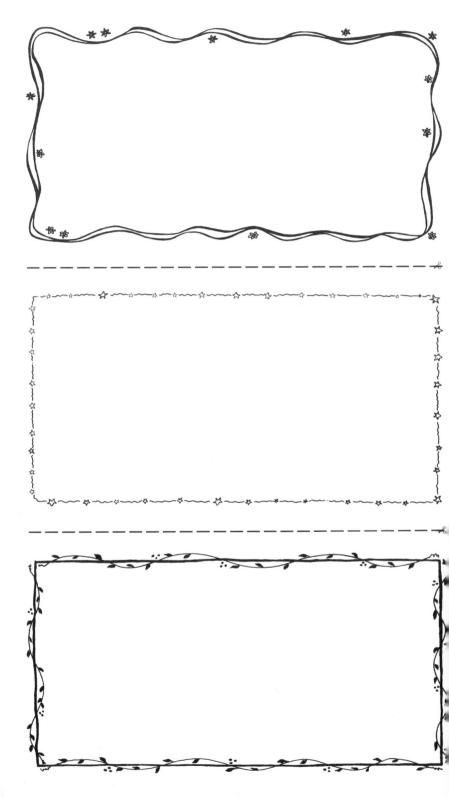

Vegetarian Black Bean Chili Mix

2 1/2 C. dried black beans

Seasoning Packet:

3 T. dried minced onion
3 T. dried minced garlic
1 tsp. dried oregano
2 tsp. salt
1/4 to 1/2 tsp. cayenne pepper

1 1/2 C. white rice in a baggie

Layer the ingredients in the order given in a wide-mouth 1-quart canning jar. Mix and place the seasonings in a small plastic bag. Place the packet on top of the beans. Place rice on top of the seasoning packet.

Attach a gift tag with the cooking directions.

Vegetarian Black Bean Chili

1 jar Vegetarian Black Bean Chili
   Mix
1 T. olive oil
1 tsp. salt

Remove baggies from the Vegetarian Black Bean Chili Mix. Wash beans. Put in large soup pot with seasonings. Add 1 tablespoon olive oil and cover beans with 2 inches of water. Bring to boil and simmer until beans are very well done (about 2 hours). Beans should be very soft. Add water as needed to keep beans from sticking. There should be some liquid left on beans when done. To cook rice, put 3 cups water and 1 teaspoon salt into a pot and when it boils, add rice. Lower heat, cover and steam for 20 minutes. Serve about 1/2 cup rice in bowl, and put beans on the top.

Vegetarian Black Bean Chili

1 jar Vegetarian Black Bean
  Chili Mix

1 T. olive oil
1 tsp. salt

Remove baggies from the Vegetarian Black Bean Chili Mix. Wash beans. Put in large soup pot with seasonings. Add 1 tablespoon olive oil and cover beans with 2 inches of water. Bring to boil and simmer until beans are very well done (about 2 hours). Beans should be very soft. Add water as needed to keep beans from sticking. There should be some liquid left on beans when done. To cook rice, put 3 cups water and 1 teaspoon salt into a pot and when it boils, add rice. Lower heat, cover and steam for 20 minutes. Serve about 1/2 cup rice in bowl, and put beans on the top.

Vegetarian Black Bean Chili

1 jar Vegetarian Black Bean
  Chili Mix

1 T. olive oil
1 tsp. salt

Remove baggies from the Vegetarian Black Bean Chili Mix. Wash beans. Put in large soup pot with seasonings. Add 1 tablespoon olive oil and cover beans with 2 inches of water. Bring to boil and simmer until beans are very well done (about 2 hours). Beans should be very soft. Add water as needed to keep beans from sticking. There should be some liquid left on beans when done. To cook rice, put 3 cups water and 1 teaspoon salt into a pot and when it boils, add rice. Lower heat, cover and steam for 20 minutes. Serve about 1/2 cup rice in bowl, and put beans on the top.

Vegetarian Black Bean Chili

1 jar Vegetarian Black Bean
  Chili Mix

1 T. olive oil
1 tsp. salt

Remove baggies from the Vegetarian Black Bean Chili Mix. Wash beans. Put in large soup pot with seasonings. Add 1 tablespoon olive oil and cover beans with 2 inches of water. Bring to boil and simmer until beans are very well done (about 2 hours). Beans should be very soft. Add water as needed to keep beans from sticking. There should be some liquid left on beans when done. To cook rice, put 3 cups water and 1 teaspoon salt into a pot and when it boils, add rice. Lower heat, cover and steam for 20 minutes. Serve about 1/2 cup rice in bowl, and put beans on the top.

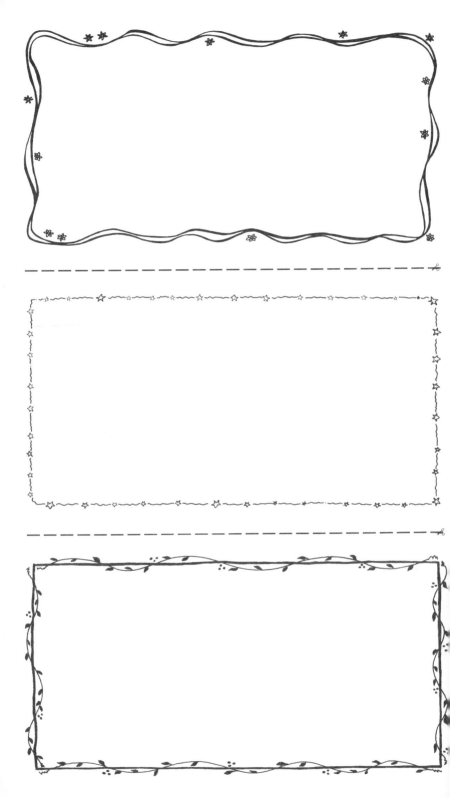

Vegetarian Black Bean Chili

1 jar Vegetarian Black Bean
  Chili Mix

1 T. olive oil
1 tsp. salt

Remove baggies from the Vegetarian Black Bean Chili Mix. Wash beans. Put in large soup pot with seasonings. Add 1 tablespoon olive oil and cover beans with 2 inches of water. Bring to boil and simmer until beans are very well done (about 2 hours). Beans should be very soft. Add water as needed to keep beans from sticking. There should be some liquid left on beans when done. To cook rice, put 3 cups water and 1 teaspoon salt into a pot and when it boils, add rice. Lower heat, cover and steam for 20 minutes. Serve about 1/2 cup rice in bowl, and put beans on the top.

Vegetarian Black Bean Chili

1 jar Vegetarian Black Bean
  Chili Mix

1 T. olive oil
1 tsp. salt

Remove baggies from the Vegetarian Black Bean Chili Mix. Wash beans. Put in large soup pot with seasonings. Add 1 tablespoon olive oil and cover beans with 2 inches of water. Bring to boil and simmer until beans are very well done (about 2 hours). Beans should be very soft. Add water as needed to keep beans from sticking. There should be some liquid left on beans when done. To cook rice, put 3 cups water and 1 teaspoon salt into a pot and when it boils, add rice. Lower heat, cover and steam for 20 minutes. Serve about 1/2 cup rice in bowl, and put beans on the top.

Vegetarian Black Bean Chili

1 jar Vegetarian Black Bean
  Chili Mix

1 T. olive oil
1 tsp. salt

Remove baggies from the Vegetarian Black Bean Chili Mix. Wash beans. Put in large soup pot with seasonings. Add 1 tablespoon olive oil and cover beans with 2 inches of water. Bring to boil and simmer until beans are very well done (about 2 hours). Beans should be very soft. Add water as needed to keep beans from sticking. There should be some liquid left on beans when done. To cook rice, put 3 cups water and 1 teaspoon salt into a pot and when it boils, add rice. Lower heat, cover and steam for 20 minutes. Serve about 1/2 cup rice in bowl, and put beans on the top.

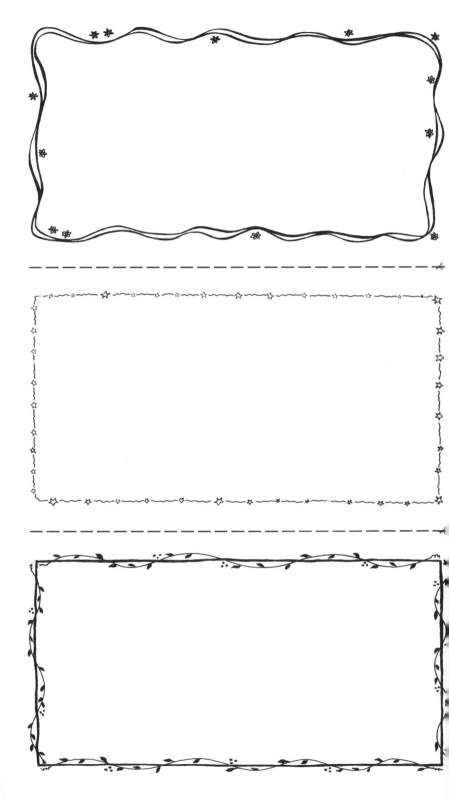

Oatmeal Cinnamon Pancake Mix

2 C. quick oats
1/2 C. brown sugar
1 C. all-purpose flour
1 C. whole wheat flour
1 T. plus 1 1/2 tsp. baking powder
1/2 C. instant dry milk
2 1/2 tsp. salt
1 T. cinnamon
1/4 tsp. cream of tartar

Layer the ingredients in the order given into a wide-mouth 1-quart canning jar. Pack each layer in place before adding the next ingredient.

Attach a gift tag with the cooking directions.

❀ *For an out of the ordinary gift, try placing the mix in a mixing bowl along with kitchen utensils, cookbooks, recipe cards, towels and pot holders.* ❀

Oatmeal Cinnamon Pancakes

Makes 10 servings

1 jar Oatmeal Cinnamon Pancake
  Mix
2/3 C. vegetable oil
4 eggs, beaten
2 C. water

Preheat a lightly greased griddle over medium low heat. In a large bowl, place the Oatmeal Cinnamon Pancake Mix. In a small bowl, beat together vegetable oil and eggs. Pour into the pancake mix, alternating with water, and mix thoroughly, creating a batter. Pour batter, 1/4 cup at a time, onto the prepared griddle. Cook on both sides until golden brown, flipping when the surface begins to bubble.

Oatmeal Cinnamon Pancakes
Makes 10 servings

1 jar Oatmeal Cinnamon
  Pancake Mix
2/3 C. vegetable oil

4 eggs, beaten
2 C. water

Preheat a lightly greased griddle over medium low heat. In a large bowl, place the Oatmeal Cinnamon Pancake Mix. In a small bowl, beat together vegetable oil and eggs. Pour into the pancake mix, alternating with water, and mix thoroughly, creating a batter. Pour batter, 1/4 cup at a time, onto the prepared griddle. Cook on both sides until golden brown, flipping when the surface begins to bubble.

Oatmeal Cinnamon Pancakes
Makes 10 servings

1 jar Oatmeal Cinnamon
  Pancake Mix
2/3 C. vegetable oil

4 eggs, beaten
2 C. water

Preheat a lightly greased griddle over medium low heat. In a large bowl, place the Oatmeal Cinnamon Pancake Mix. In a small bowl, beat together vegetable oil and eggs. Pour into the pancake mix, alternating with water, and mix thoroughly, creating a batter. Pour batter, 1/4 cup at a time, onto the prepared griddle. Cook on both sides until golden brown, flipping when the surface begins to bubble.

Oatmeal Cinnamon Pancakes
Makes 10 servings

1 jar Oatmeal Cinnamon
  Pancake Mix
2/3 C. vegetable oil

4 eggs, beaten
2 C. water

Preheat a lightly greased griddle over medium low heat. In a large bowl, place the Oatmeal Cinnamon Pancake Mix. In a small bowl, beat together vegetable oil and eggs. Pour into the pancake mix, alternating with water, and mix thoroughly, creating a batter. Pour batter, 1/4 cup at a time, onto the prepared griddle. Cook on both sides until golden brown, flipping when the surface begins to bubble.

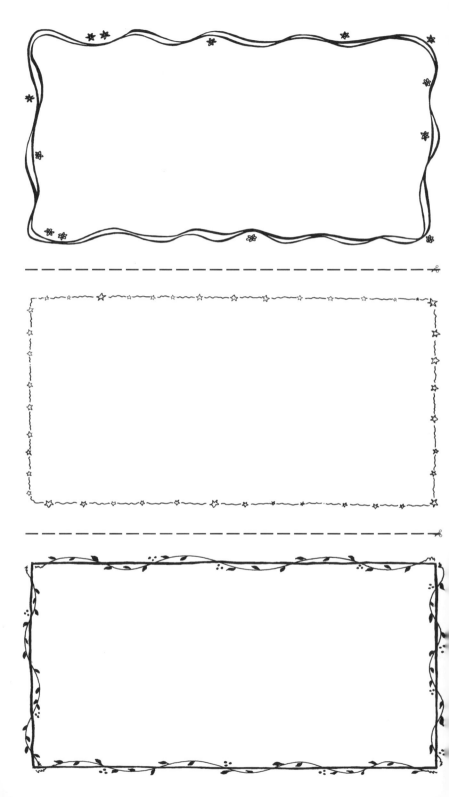

Oatmeal Cinnamon Pancakes
Makes 10 servings

1 jar Oatmeal Cinnamon
  Pancake Mix
2/3 C. vegetable oil

4 eggs, beaten
2 C. water

Preheat a lightly greased griddle over medium low heat. In a large bowl, place the Oatmeal Cinnamon Pancake Mix. In a small bowl, beat together vegetable oil and eggs. Pour into the pancake mix, alternating with water, and mix thoroughly, creating a batter. Pour batter, 1/4 cup at a time, onto the prepared griddle. Cook on both sides until golden brown, flipping when the surface begins to bubble.

Oatmeal Cinnamon Pancakes
Makes 10 servings

1 jar Oatmeal Cinnamon
  Pancake Mix
2/3 C. vegetable oil

4 eggs, beaten
2 C. water

Preheat a lightly greased griddle over medium low heat. In a large bowl, place the Oatmeal Cinnamon Pancake Mix. In a small bowl, beat together vegetable oil and eggs. Pour into the pancake mix, alternating with water, and mix thoroughly, creating a batter. Pour batter, 1/4 cup at a time, onto the prepared griddle. Cook on both sides until golden brown, flipping when the surface begins to bubble.

Oatmeal Cinnamon Pancakes
Makes 10 servings

1 jar Oatmeal Cinnamon
  Pancake Mix
2/3 C. vegetable oil

4 eggs, beaten
2 C. water

Preheat a lightly greased griddle over medium low heat. In a large bowl, place the Oatmeal Cinnamon Pancake Mix. In a small bowl, beat together vegetable oil and eggs. Pour into the pancake mix, alternating with water, and mix thoroughly, creating a batter. Pour batter, 1/4 cup at a time, onto the prepared griddle. Cook on both sides until golden brown, flipping when the surface begins to bubble.

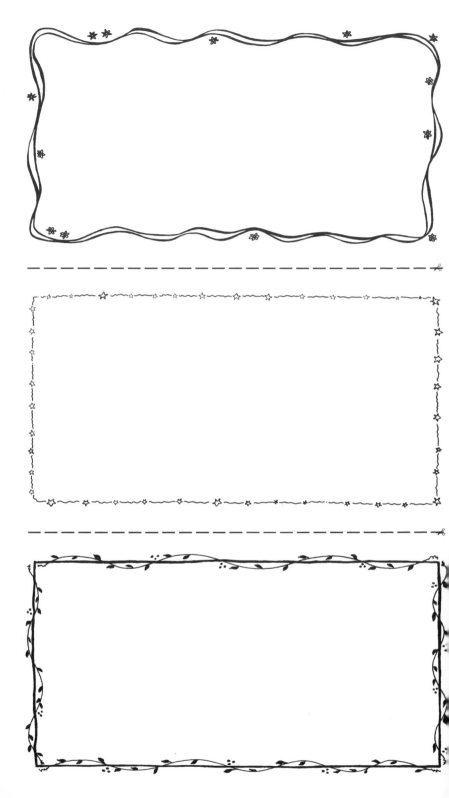

Ground Beef Stroganoff Mix

1/2 C. plus 2 T. instant dry milk
1/3 C. cornstarch
1 T. plus 1 tsp. chicken or beef
   bouillon granules
2 tsp. dried minced onion
1/4 tsp. plus 1/8 tsp. dried basil
1/4 tsp. plus 1/8 tsp. dried
   thyme
1/4 tsp. plus 1/8 tsp. pepper
2 tsp. dried parsley flakes
1 tsp. garlic powder
2 C. egg noodles

Layer the ingredients in the order given into a wide-mouth 1-quart canning jar. Pack each layer into place before adding the next ingredient.

Attach a gift tag with the cooking directions.

Ground Beef Stroganoff

Makes 5 servings

1 jar Ground Beef Stroganoff
   Mix
1 1/2 lbs. ground beef
4 C. water
1 C. sour cream

In a large skillet, brown ground beef and drain off fat. Add 4 cups of water and the Ground Beef Stroganoff Mix to skillet and stir. Bring mixture to a boil, reduce heat, cover and simmer for 15 to 20 minutes or until noodles are tender. Top with sour cream and serve immediately.

Ground Beef Stroganoff

Makes 5 servings

1 jar Ground Beef Stroganoff
  Mix
1 1/2 lbs. ground beef

4 C. water
1 C. sour cream

In a large skillet, brown ground beef and drain off fat. Add 4 cups of water and the Ground Beef Stroganoff Mix to skillet and stir. Bring mixture to a boil, reduce heat, cover and simmer for 15 to 20 minutes or until noodles are tender. Top with sour cream and serve immediately.

Ground Beef Stroganoff

Makes 5 servings

1 jar Ground Beef Stroganoff
  Mix
1 1/2 lbs. ground beef

4 C. water
1 C. sour cream

In a large skillet, brown ground beef and drain off fat. Add 4 cups of water and the Ground Beef Stroganoff Mix to skillet and stir. Bring mixture to a boil, reduce heat, cover and simmer for 15 to 20 minutes or until noodles are tender. Top with sour cream and serve immediately.

Ground Beef Stroganoff

Makes 5 servings

1 jar Ground Beef Stroganoff
  Mix
1 1/2 lbs. ground beef

4 C. water
1 C. sour cream

In a large skillet, brown ground beef and drain off fat. Add 4 cups of water and the Ground Beef Stroganoff Mix to skillet and stir. Bring mixture to a boil, reduce heat, cover and simmer for 15 to 20 minutes or until noodles are tender. Top with sour cream and serve immediately.

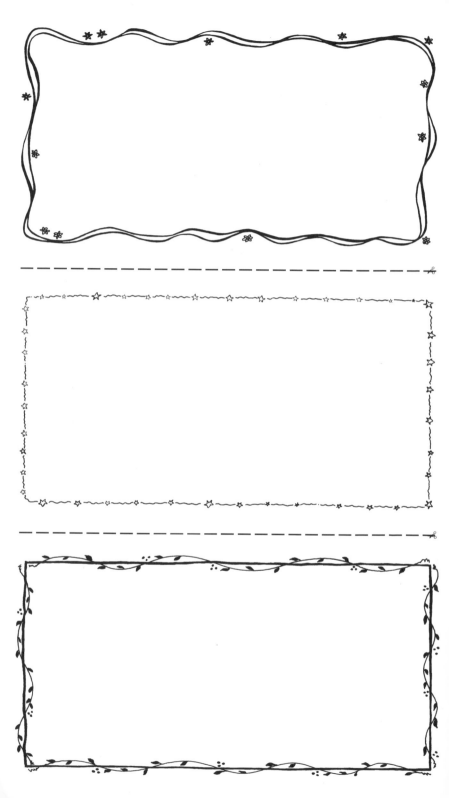

Ground Beef Stroganoff
Makes 5 servings

1 jar Ground Beef Stroganoff
  Mix
1 1/2 lbs. ground beef

4 C. water
1 C. sour cream

    In a large skillet, brown ground beef and drain off fat. Add 4 cups of water and the Ground Beef Stroganoff Mix to skillet and stir. Bring mixture to a boil, reduce heat, cover and simmer for 15 to 20 minutes or until noodles are tender. Top with sour cream and serve immediately.

Ground Beef Stroganoff
Makes 5 servings

1 jar Ground Beef Stroganoff
  Mix
1 1/2 lbs. ground beef

4 C. water
1 C. sour cream

    In a large skillet, brown ground beef and drain off fat. Add 4 cups of water and the Ground Beef Stroganoff Mix to skillet and stir. Bring mixture to a boil, reduce heat, cover and simmer for 15 to 20 minutes or until noodles are tender. Top with sour cream and serve immediately.

Ground Beef Stroganoff
Makes 5 servings

1 jar Ground Beef Stroganoff
  Mix
1 1/2 lbs. ground beef

4 C. water
1 C. sour cream

    In a large skillet, brown ground beef and drain off fat. Add 4 cups of water and the Ground Beef Stroganoff Mix to skillet and stir. Bring mixture to a boil, reduce heat, cover and simmer for 15 to 20 minutes or until noodles are tender. Top with sour cream and serve immediately.

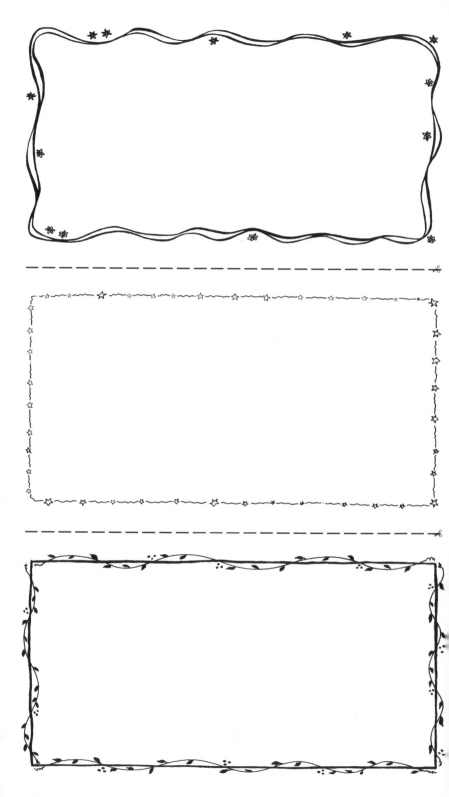

Skillet Lasagna Mix

1/4 C. plus 2 T. instant dry milk
2 T. plus 2 tsp. cornstarch
2 tsp. chicken or beef
  bouillon granules
1/4 tsp. dried basil
1/4 tsp. dried thyme
1/4 tsp. pepper
1 tsp. dried parsley flakes
1/2 tsp. garlic powder
1/4 C. dried minced onion
1/4 C. Parmesan cheese
3 C. egg noodles

Layer the ingredients in the order given into a wide-mouth 1-quart canning jar. Pack each layer in place before adding the next ingredient.

Attach a gift tag with the cooking directions.

Skillet Lasagna

Makes about 6 servings

1 jar Skillet Lasagna Mix
1 lb. ground beef
2 C. water
1 (16 oz.) can tomato sauce
2 C. mozzarella cheese

In a large skillet, brown ground beef and crumble. Drain off fat and add Skillet Lasagna Mix, water and tomato sauce. Bring to a boil. Reduce heat and simmer for 15 minutes, stirring until thickened. Top with mozzarella cheese 5 minutes before serving. Turn off heat, stop stirring and allow cheese to melt.

Skillet Lasagna
Makes about 6 servings

1 jar Skillet Lasagna Mix
1 lb. ground beef
2 C. mozzarella cheese

2 C. water
1 (16 oz.) can tomato sauce

In a large skillet, brown ground beef and crumble. Drain off fat and add Skillet Lasagna Mix, water and tomato sauce. Bring to a boil. Reduce heat and simmer for 15 minutes, stirring until thickened. Top with mozzarella cheese 5 minutes before serving. Turn off heat, stop stirring and allow cheese to melt.

Skillet Lasagna
Makes about 6 servings

1 jar Skillet Lasagna Mix
1 lb. ground beef
2 C. mozzarella cheese

2 C. water
1 (16 oz.) can tomato sauce

In a large skillet, brown ground beef and crumble. Drain off fat and add Skillet Lasagna Mix, water and tomato sauce. Bring to a boil. Reduce heat and simmer for 15 minutes, stirring until thickened. Top with mozzarella cheese 5 minutes before serving. Turn off heat, stop stirring and allow cheese to melt.

Skillet Lasagna
Makes about 6 servings

1 jar Skillet Lasagna Mix
1 lb. ground beef
2 C. mozzarella cheese

2 C. water
1 (16 oz.) can tomato sauce

In a large skillet, brown ground beef and crumble. Drain off fat and add Skillet Lasagna Mix, water and tomato sauce. Bring to a boil. Reduce heat and simmer for 15 minutes, stirring until thickened. Top with mozzarella cheese 5 minutes before serving. Turn off heat, stop stirring and allow cheese to melt.

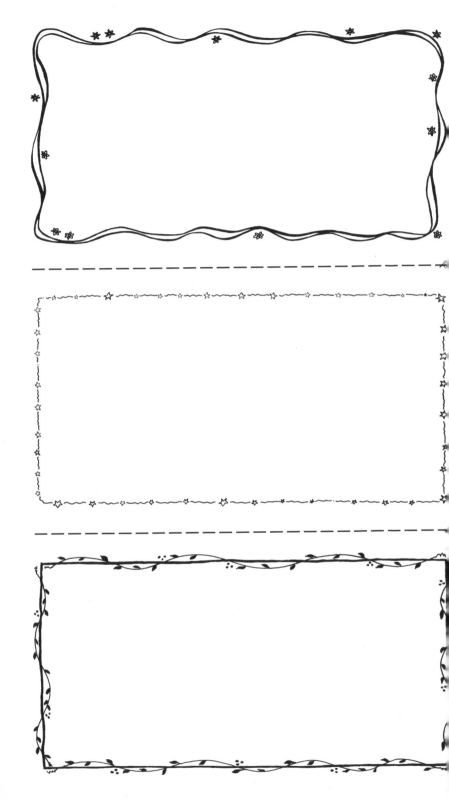

Creamy Wild Rice & Mushroom Soup Mix

2 (2.75 oz.) pkgs. country gravy
  mix
2 T. chicken bouillon granules
1 T. plus 1 tsp. dried minced
  onion
1 T. plus 1 tsp. dried celery flakes
2 tsp. dried parsley flakes
1/2 C. wild rice
1 1/4 C. white rice

Layer the ingredients in the order given into a wide-mouth 1-quart canning jar. Pack each layer in place before adding the next ingredient.

Attach a gift tag with the cooking directions.

❈ *Small appliques or embroidery can be added to the center of a fabric cover to further personalize the gift.* ❈

Creamy Wild Rice & Mushroom Soup

Makes 12 servings

1 jar Creamy Wild Rice &
  Mushroom Soup Mix
1 (4 oz.) can mushrooms
14 C. water

Place Creamy Wild Rice & Mushroom Soup Mix into a large soup pot. Add mushrooms and 14 cups of water. Heat to boiling, reduce heat, cover and simmer for 25 to 30 minutes or until rice is tender, stirring occasionally.

Creamy Wild Rice & Mushroom Soup
Makes 12 servings

1 jar Creamy Wild Rice &
   Mushroom Soup Mix

1 (4 oz.) can mushrooms
14 C. water

    Place Creamy Wild Rice & Mushroom Soup Mix into a large soup pot. Add mushrooms and 14 cups of water. Heat to boiling, reduce heat, cover and simmer for 25 to 30 minutes or until rice is tender, stirring occasionally.

Creamy Wild Rice & Mushroom Soup
Makes 12 servings

1 jar Creamy Wild Rice &
   Mushroom Soup Mix

1 (4 oz.) can mushrooms
14 C. water

    Place Creamy Wild Rice & Mushroom Soup Mix into a large soup pot. Add mushrooms and 14 cups of water. Heat to boiling, reduce heat, cover and simmer for 25 to 30 minutes or until rice is tender, stirring occasionally.

Creamy Wild Rice & Mushroom Soup
Makes 12 servings

1 jar Creamy Wild Rice &
   Mushroom Soup Mix

1 (4 oz.) can mushrooms
14 C. water

    Place Creamy Wild Rice & Mushroom Soup Mix into a large soup pot. Add mushrooms and 14 cups of water. Heat to boiling, reduce heat, cover and simmer for 25 to 30 minutes or until rice is tender, stirring occasionally.

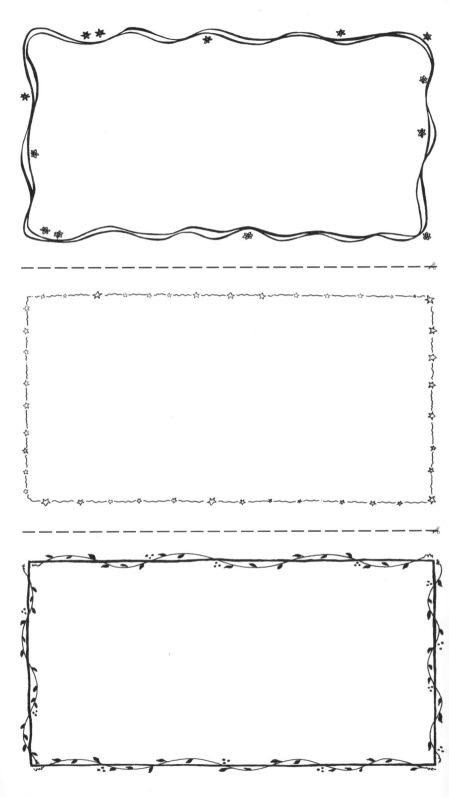

Creamy Wild Rice & Mushroom Soup
Makes 12 servings

1 jar Creamy Wild Rice &
  Mushroom Soup Mix

1 (4 oz.) can mushrooms
14 C. water

    Place Creamy Wild Rice & Mushroom Soup Mix into a large soup pot. Add mushrooms and 14 cups of water. Heat to boiling, reduce heat, cover and simmer for 25 to 30 minutes or until rice is tender, stirring occasionally.

Creamy Wild Rice & Mushroom Soup
Makes 12 servings

1 jar Creamy Wild Rice &
  Mushroom Soup Mix

1 (4 oz.) can mushrooms
14 C. water

    Place Creamy Wild Rice & Mushroom Soup Mix into a large soup pot. Add mushrooms and 14 cups of water. Heat to boiling, reduce heat, cover and simmer for 25 to 30 minutes or until rice is tender, stirring occasionally.

Creamy Wild Rice & Mushroom Soup
Makes 12 servings

1 jar Creamy Wild Rice &
  Mushroom Soup Mix

1 (4 oz.) can mushrooms
14 C. water

    Place Creamy Wild Rice & Mushroom Soup Mix into a large soup pot. Add mushrooms and 14 cups of water. Heat to boiling, reduce heat, cover and simmer for 25 to 30 minutes or until rice is tender, stirring occasionally.

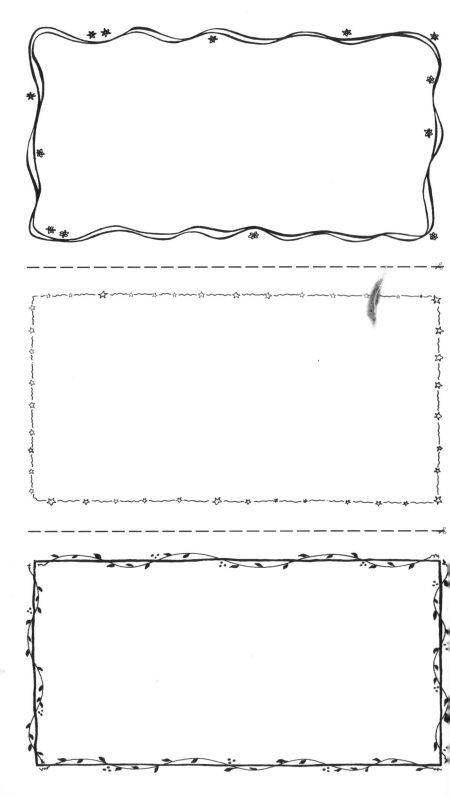

Texas Two-Step Soup Mix

2 (1.61 oz.) pkgs. country brown
    gravy mix
1/4 C. chili powder
1 T. plus 1 tsp. dried oregano
2 tsp. ground cumin
2 tsp. dried minced onion
1 tsp. garlic salt
22 to 24 tortilla chips, coarsely
    crushed
2 1/3 C. small to medium sized
    pasta (wheels, shells,
    macaroni, etc.)

Layer the ingredients in the order given into a wide-mouth 1-quart canning jar. Pack each layer in place before adding the next ingredient.

Attach a gift tag with the cooking directions.

Texas Two-Step Soup

Makes 16 servings

1 jar Texas Two-Step Soup Mix
1 lb. ground beef
14 C. water
1 (15 oz.) can corn with red and
   green bell peppers
2 (16 oz.) cans chopped
   tomatoes

Brown ground beef in a large soup pot. Add Texas Two-Step Soup Mix and water; heat to boiling. Stir in corn and tomatoes. Reduce heat, cover and simmer for 20 to 25 minutes or until pasta is tender, stirring occasionally. Serve with additional crushed tortilla chips and shredded Monterey Jack cheese, if desired.

Texas Two-Step Soup

Makes 16 servings

1 jar Texas Two-Step Soup Mix
1 lb. ground beef
14 C. water

1 (15 oz.) can corn with red and
   green bell peppers
2 (16 oz.) cans chopped tomatoes

Brown ground beef in a large soup pot. Add Texas Two-Step Soup Mix and water; heat to boiling. Stir in corn and tomatoes. Reduce heat, cover and simmer for 20 to 25 minutes or until pasta is tender, stirring occasionally. Serve with additional crushed tortilla chips and shredded Monterey Jack cheese, if desired.

Texas Two-Step Soup

Makes 16 servings

1 jar Texas Two-Step Soup Mix
1 lb. ground beef
14 C. water

1 (15 oz.) can corn with red and
   green bell peppers
2 (16 oz.) cans chopped tomatoes

Brown ground beef in a large soup pot. Add Texas Two-Step Soup Mix and water; heat to boiling. Stir in corn and tomatoes. Reduce heat, cover and simmer for 20 to 25 minutes or until pasta is tender, stirring occasionally. Serve with additional crushed tortilla chips and shredded Monterey Jack cheese, if desired.

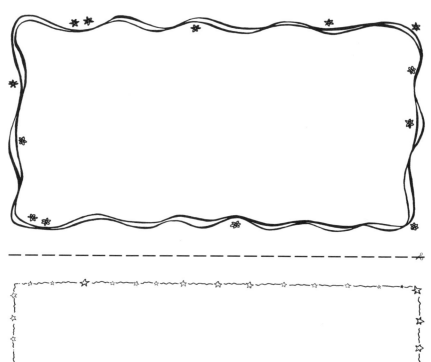

Texas Two-Step Soup

Makes 16 servings

1 jar Texas Two-Step Soup Mix
1 lb. ground beef
14 C. water

1 (15 oz.) can corn with red and
green bell peppers
2 (16 oz.) cans chopped tomatoes

Brown ground beef in a large soup pot. Add Texas Two-Step Soup Mix and water; heat to boiling. Stir in corn and tomatoes. Reduce heat, cover and simmer for 20 to 25 minutes or until pasta is tender, stirring occasionally. Serve with additional crushed tortilla chips and shredded Monterey Jack cheese, if desired.

Texas Two-Step Soup

Makes 16 servings

1 jar Texas Two-Step Soup Mix
1 lb. ground beef
14 C. water

1 (15 oz.) can corn with red and
green bell peppers
2 (16 oz.) cans chopped tomatoes

Brown ground beef in a large soup pot. Add Texas Two-Step Soup Mix and water; heat to boiling. Stir in corn and tomatoes. Reduce heat, cover and simmer for 20 to 25 minutes or until pasta is tender, stirring occasionally. Serve with additional crushed tortilla chips and shredded Monterey Jack cheese, if desired.

Texas Two-Step Soup

Makes 16 servings

1 jar Texas Two-Step Soup Mix
1 lb. ground beef
14 C. water

1 (15 oz.) can corn with red and
green bell peppers
2 (16 oz.) cans chopped tomatoes

Brown ground beef in a large soup pot. Add Texas Two-Step Soup Mix and water; heat to boiling. Stir in corn and tomatoes. Reduce heat, cover and simmer for 20 to 25 minutes or until pasta is tender, stirring occasionally. Serve with additional crushed tortilla chips and shredded Monterey Jack cheese, if desired.

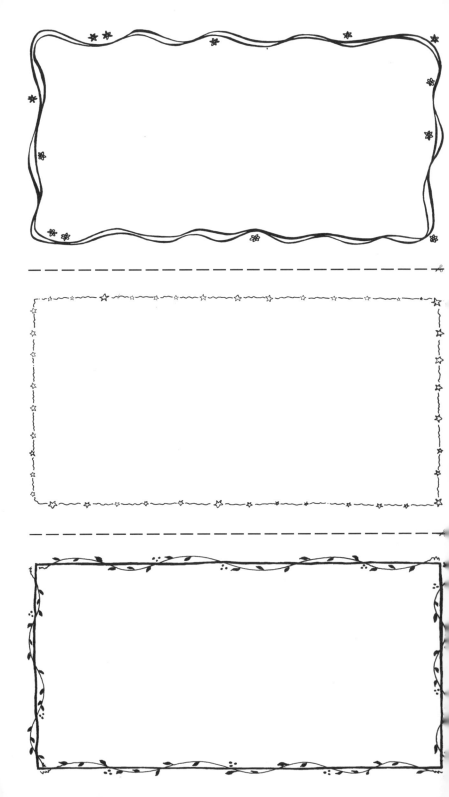

Beef & Noodle Quick Dinner Mix

2/3 C. instant dry milk
2 tsp. onion powder
2 tsp. garlic powder
1/2 tsp. plus 1/8 tsp. pepper
1/2 tsp. plus 1/8 tsp. salt
1/8 tsp. dried basil
1/8 tsp. dried oregano
1/2 tsp. plus 1/8 tsp. paprika
Pinch cayenne pepper
2 T. plus 2 tsp. brown gravy mix
1/8 tsp. celery seed
1 T. plus 1 tsp. cornstarch
3 C. egg noodles

Layer the ingredients in the order given into a wide-mouth 1-quart canning jar. Pack each layer in place before adding the next ingredient.

Attach a gift tag with the cooking directions.

Beef & Noodle Quick Dinner

1 jar Beef & Noodle Quick
 Dinner Mix
1 1/2 lbs. ground beef
1 (4 oz.) can mushrooms
7 C. water

Brown ground beef in a large skillet. Drain excess fat. Add the mushrooms and water. Stir in Beef & Noodle Quick Dinner Mix and bring to a boil. Reduce heat to simmer, cover and cook approximately 15 minutes. Remove lid and let gently simmer until sauce has thickened to desired amount. You may wish to leave the sauce a little soupy as it will thicken as it sits.

Beef & Noodle Quick Dinner

1 jar Beef & Noodle Quick
  Dinner Mix
1 1/2 lbs. ground beef

1 (4 oz.) can mushrooms
7 C. water

Brown ground beef in a large skillet. Drain excess fat. Add the mushrooms and water. Stir in Beef & Noodle Quick Dinner Mix and bring to a boil. Reduce heat to simmer, cover and cook approximately 15 minutes. Remove lid and let gently simmer until sauce has thickened to desired amount. You may wish to leave the sauce a little soupy as it will thicken as it sits.

Beef & Noodle Quick Dinner

1 jar Beef & Noodle Quick
  Dinner Mix
1 1/2 lbs. ground beef

1 (4 oz.) can mushrooms
7 C. water

Brown ground beef in a large skillet. Drain excess fat. Add the mushrooms and water. Stir in Beef & Noodle Quick Dinner Mix and bring to a boil. Reduce heat to simmer, cover and cook approximately 15 minutes. Remove lid and let gently simmer until sauce has thickened to desired amount. You may wish to leave the sauce a little soupy as it will thicken as it sits.

Beef & Noodle Quick Dinner

1 jar Beef & Noodle Quick
  Dinner Mix
1 1/2 lbs. ground beef

1 (4 oz.) can mushrooms
7 C. water

Brown ground beef in a large skillet. Drain excess fat. Add the mushrooms and water. Stir in Beef & Noodle Quick Dinner Mix and bring to a boil. Reduce heat to simmer, cover and cook approximately 15 minutes. Remove lid and let gently simmer until sauce has thickened to desired amount. You may wish to leave the sauce a little soupy as it will thicken as it sits.

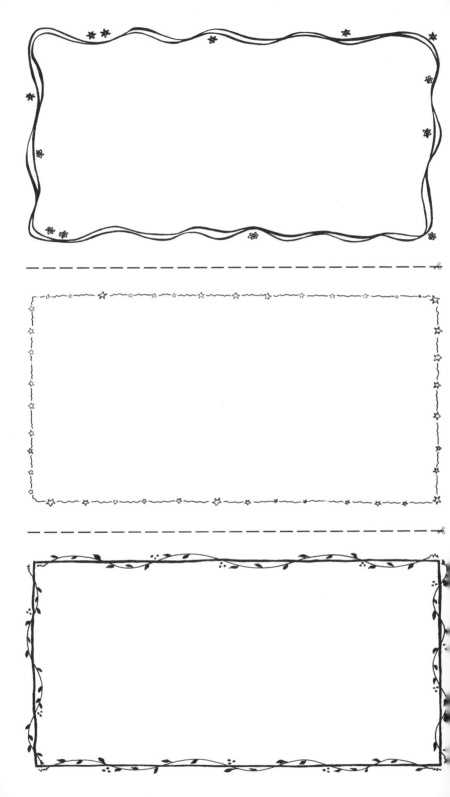

Beef & Noodle Quick Dinner

1 jar Beef & Noodle Quick
  Dinner Mix
1 1/2 lbs. ground beef

1 (4 oz.) can mushrooms
7 C. water

Brown ground beef in a large skillet. Drain excess fat. Add the mushrooms and water. Stir in Beef & Noodle Quick Dinner Mix and bring to a boil. Reduce heat to simmer, cover and cook approximately 15 minutes. Remove lid and let gently simmer until sauce has thickened to desired amount. You may wish to leave the sauce a little soupy as it will thicken as it sits.

Beef & Noodle Quick Dinner

1 jar Beef & Noodle Quick
  Dinner Mix
1 1/2 lbs. ground beef

1 (4 oz.) can mushrooms
7 C. water

Brown ground beef in a large skillet. Drain excess fat. Add the mushrooms and water. Stir in Beef & Noodle Quick Dinner Mix and bring to a boil. Reduce heat to simmer, cover and cook approximately 15 minutes. Remove lid and let gently simmer until sauce has thickened to desired amount. You may wish to leave the sauce a little soupy as it will thicken as it sits.

Beef & Noodle Quick Dinner

1 jar Beef & Noodle Quick
  Dinner Mix
1 1/2 lbs. ground beef

1 (4 oz.) can mushrooms
7 C. water

Brown ground beef in a large skillet. Drain excess fat. Add the mushrooms and water. Stir in Beef & Noodle Quick Dinner Mix and bring to a boil. Reduce heat to simmer, cover and cook approximately 15 minutes. Remove lid and let gently simmer until sauce has thickened to desired amount. You may wish to leave the sauce a little soupy as it will thicken as it sits.

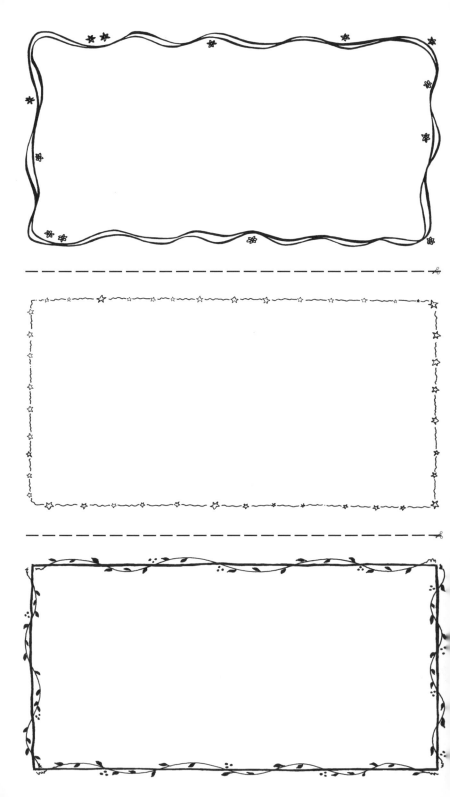

Painted Desert Chili Mix

1/4 C. dried parsley
  flakes
2 T. garlic powder
2 T. taco seasoning
2 T. dried minced
  onion
2 T. taco seasoning
2 T. cumin
2 T. paprika
2 T. white or yellow
  cornmeal
2 T. taco seasoning

2 T. garlic powder
2 T. chili powder
2 T. dried parsley
  flakes
1 C. dried pinto
  beans
1/4 C. small dried
  white beans
1/4 C. small dried
  black beans
Approximately 1 C.
  dried kidney beans

Layer the ingredients in the order given into a wide-mouth 1-quart canning jar. The desert effect comes from the rippled appearance of the spices. Carefully add each seasoning along the edges of the jar, then fill the middle of the layer. Pack each layer in place before adding the next ingredient.

Attach a gift tag with the cooking directions.

Painted Desert Chili

1 jar Painted Desert Chili Mix
1 medium onion, diced
1/2 C. cider vinegar
1/2 C. brown sugar
1 (49 oz.) can tomato juice
2 lbs. ground beef, browned
4 (15 oz.) cans diced tomatoes
1 (12 oz.) can tomato paste
20 C. water
Salt and pepper to taste

Place Painted Desert Chili Mix into a large soup pot. Add onion, cider vinegar, brown sugar, tomato juice, browned ground beef and water. Bring to a boil, reduce heat and simmer for 2 to 2 1/2 hours or until beans are tender. Add diced tomatoes and tomato paste and continue simmering for another 1/2 hour. Add salt and pepper to taste.

Painted Desert Chili

1 jar Painted Desert Chili Mix
1 medium onion, diced
1/2 C. cider vinegar
1/2 C. brown sugar
1 (49 oz.) can tomato juice
2 lbs. ground beef, browned

4 (15 oz.) cans diced
  tomatoes
1 (12 oz.) can tomato paste
20 C. water
Salt and pepper to taste

Place Painted Desert Chili Mix into a large stock pot. Add onion, cider vinegar, brown sugar, tomato juice, browned ground beef and water. Bring to a boil, reduce heat and simmer for 2 to 2 1/2 hours or until beans are tender. Add diced tomatoes and tomato paste and continue simmering for another 1/2 hour. Add salt and pepper to taste.

Painted Desert Chili

1 jar Painted Desert Chili Mix
1 medium onion, diced
1/2 C. cider vinegar
1/2 C. brown sugar
1 (49 oz.) can tomato juice
2 lbs. ground beef, browned

4 (15 oz.) cans diced
  tomatoes
1 (12 oz.) can tomato paste
20 C. water
Salt and pepper to taste

Place Painted Desert Chili Mix into a large stock pot. Add onion, cider vinegar, brown sugar, tomato juice, browned ground beef and water. Bring to a boil, reduce heat and simmer for 2 to 2 1/2 hours or until beans are tender. Add diced tomatoes and tomato paste and continue simmering for another 1/2 hour. Add salt and pepper to taste.

Painted Desert Chili

1 jar Painted Desert Chili Mix
1 medium onion, diced
1/2 C. cider vinegar
1/2 C. brown sugar
1 (49 oz.) can tomato juice
2 lbs. ground beef, browned

4 (15 oz.) cans diced
  tomatoes
1 (12 oz.) can tomato paste
20 C. water
Salt and pepper to taste

Place Painted Desert Chili Mix into a large stock pot. Add onion, cider vinegar, brown sugar, tomato juice, browned ground beef and water. Bring to a boil, reduce heat and simmer for 2 to 2 1/2 hours or until beans are tender. Add diced tomatoes and tomato paste and continue simmering for another 1/2 hour. Add salt and pepper to taste.

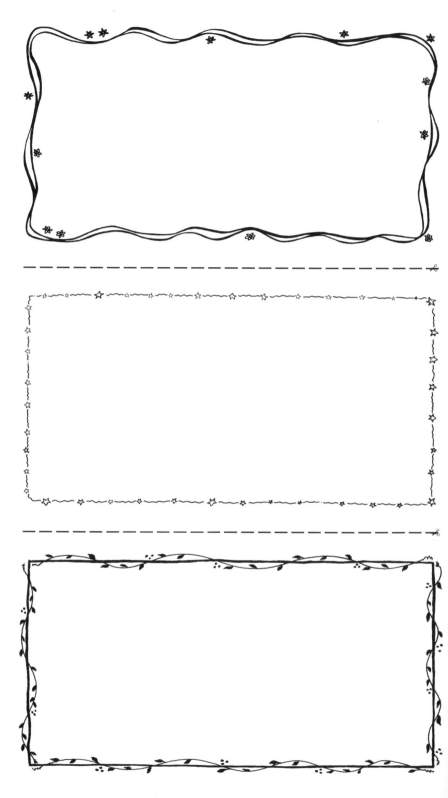

Painted Desert Chili

1 jar Painted Desert Chili Mix
1 medium onion, diced
1/2 C. cider vinegar
1/2 C. brown sugar
1 (49 oz.) can tomato juice
2 lbs. ground beef, browned

4 (15 oz.) cans diced
   tomatoes
1 (12 oz.) can tomato paste
20 C. water
Salt and pepper to taste

Place Painted Desert Chili Mix into a large stock pot. Add onion, cider vinegar, brown sugar, tomato juice, browned ground beef and water. Bring to a boil, reduce heat and simmer for 2 to 2 1/2 hours or until beans are tender. Add diced tomatoes and tomato paste and continue simmering for another 1/2 hour. Add salt and pepper to taste.

Painted Desert Chili

1 jar Painted Desert Chili Mix
1 medium onion, diced
1/2 C. cider vinegar
1/2 C. brown sugar
1 (49 oz.) can tomato juice
2 lbs. ground beef, browned

4 (15 oz.) cans diced
   tomatoes
1 (12 oz.) can tomato paste
20 C. water
Salt and pepper to taste

Place Painted Desert Chili Mix into a large stock pot. Add onion, cider vinegar, brown sugar, tomato juice, browned ground beef and water. Bring to a boil, reduce heat and simmer for 2 to 2 1/2 hours or until beans are tender. Add diced tomatoes and tomato paste and continue simmering for another 1/2 hour. Add salt and pepper to taste.

Painted Desert Chili

1 jar Painted Desert Chili Mix
1 medium onion, diced
1/2 C. cider vinegar
1/2 C. brown sugar
1 (49 oz.) can tomato juice
2 lbs. ground beef, browned

4 (15 oz.) cans diced
   tomatoes
1 (12 oz.) can tomato paste
20 C. water
Salt and pepper to taste

Place Painted Desert Chili Mix into a large stock pot. Add onion, cider vinegar, brown sugar, tomato juice, browned ground beef and water. Bring to a boil, reduce heat and simmer for 2 to 2 1/2 hours or until beans are tender. Add diced tomatoes and tomato paste and continue simmering for another 1/2 hour. Add salt and pepper to taste.

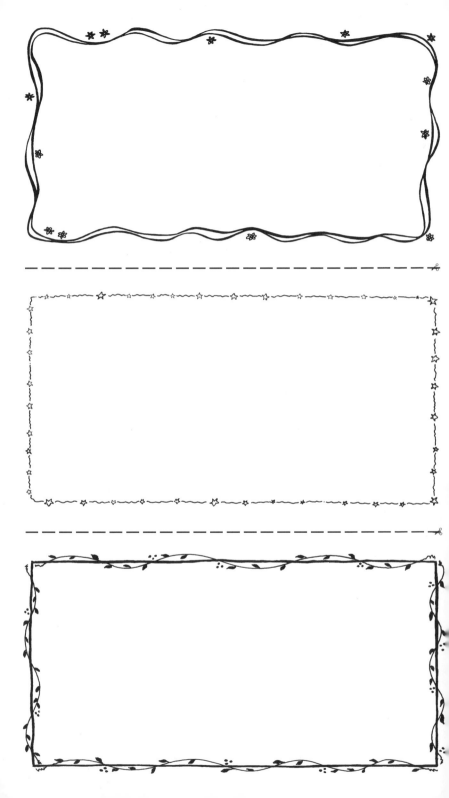

Chicken Rice Soup Mix

3 C. long-grain brown rice
3/4 C. chicken bouillon granules
2 T. dried tarragon
2 T. dried parsley flakes
1/2 tsp. pepper

Layer the ingredients in the order given into a wide-mouth 1-quart canning jar. Pack each layer in place before adding the next ingredient.

Attach a gift tag with the cooking directions.

❀ *At times, it may seem impossible to make all of the jar ingredients fit, but with persistence, they do all fit.* ❀

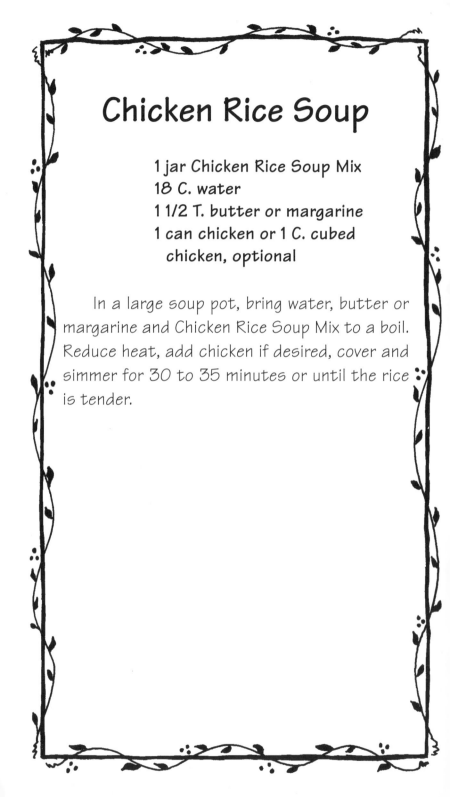

Chicken Rice Soup

1 jar Chicken Rice Soup Mix
18 C. water
1 1/2 T. butter or margarine
1 can chicken or 1 C. cubed
   chicken, optional

   In a large soup pot, bring water, butter or margarine and Chicken Rice Soup Mix to a boil. Reduce heat, add chicken if desired, cover and simmer for 30 to 35 minutes or until the rice is tender.

Chicken Rice Soup

1 jar Chicken Rice Soup Mix
18 C. water
1 1/2 T. butter or margarine

1 can chicken or 1 C. cubed
chicken, optional

In a large soup pot, bring water, butter or margarine and Chicken Rice Soup Mix to a boil. Reduce heat, add chicken if desired, cover and simmer for 30 to 35 minutes or until the rice is tender.

Chicken Rice Soup

1 jar Chicken Rice Soup Mix
18 C. water
1 1/2 T. butter or margarine

1 can chicken or 1 C. cubed
chicken, optional

In a large soup pot, bring water, butter or margarine and Chicken Rice Soup Mix to a boil. Reduce heat, add chicken if desired, cover and simmer for 30 to 35 minutes or until the rice is tender.

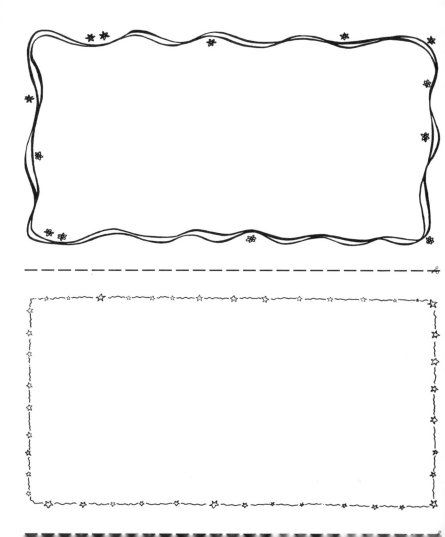

Chicken Rice Soup

1 jar Chicken Rice Soup Mix
18 C. water
1 1/2 T. butter or margarine

1 can chicken or 1 C. cubed
chicken, optional

In a large soup pot, bring water, butter or margarine and Chicken Rice Soup Mix to a boil. Reduce heat, add chicken if desired, cover and simmer for 30 to 35 minutes or until the rice is tender.

Chicken Rice Soup

1 jar Chicken Rice Soup Mix
18 C. water
1 1/2 T. butter or margarine

1 can chicken or 1 C. cubed
chicken, optional

In a large soup pot, bring water, butter or margarine and Chicken Rice Soup Mix to a boil. Reduce heat, add chicken if desired, cover and simmer for 30 to 35 minutes or until the rice is tender.

Chicken Rice Soup

1 jar Chicken Rice Soup Mix
18 C. water
1 1/2 T. butter or margarine

1 can chicken or 1 C. cubed
chicken, optional

In a large soup pot, bring water, butter or margarine and Chicken Rice Soup Mix to a boil. Reduce heat, add chicken if desired, cover and simmer for 30 to 35 minutes or until the rice is tender.

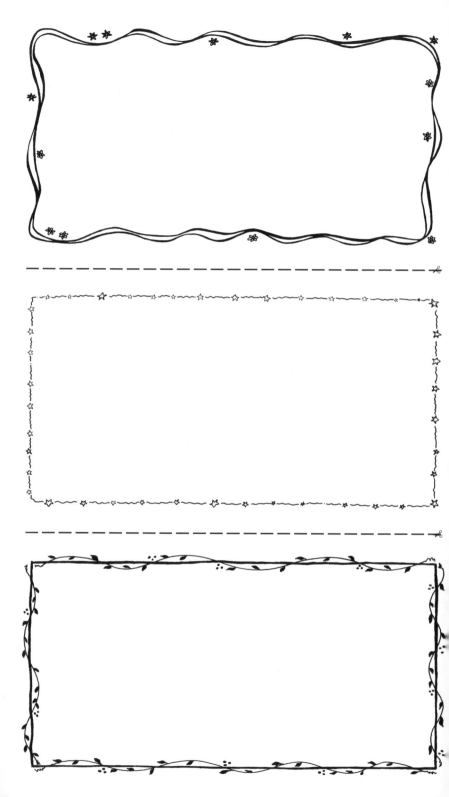

Santa Fe Skillet Casserole Mix

4 C. Fritos corn chips
1 pkg. taco seasoning
2 tsp. chicken bouillon granules
3/4 C. Parmesan cheese
1/4 C. instant dry milk
1/4 C. all-purpose flour

Layer the ingredients in the order given into a wide-mouth 1-quart canning jar. Pack each layer in place before adding the next ingredient.

Attach a gift tag with the cooking directions.

For a special touch, attach a wooden spoon to the jar.

Santa Fe Skillet Casserole

1 jar Santa Fe Skillet Casserole
  Mix
1 lb. ground beef
2 C. water
1 (4.5 oz.) can chopped green
  chilies, drained, optional

In a large skillet, brown ground beef and drain off fat. Add water and Santa Fe Skillet Casserole Mix and stir until the mixture is well blended. Cook over medium-high heat until sauce thickens. If desired, add green chilies and heat through.

Santa Fe Skillet Casserole

1 jar Santa Fe Skillet
  Casserole Mix
1 lb. ground beef

2 C. water
1 (4.5 oz.) can chopped green
  chilies, drained, optional

In a large skillet, brown ground beef and drain off fat. Add water and Santa Fe Skillet Casserole Mix and stir until the mixture is well blended. Cook over medium-high heat until sauce thickens. If desired, add green chilies and heat through.

Santa Fe Skillet Casserole

1 jar Santa Fe Skillet
  Casserole Mix
1 lb. ground beef

2 C. water
1 (4.5 oz.) can chopped green
  chilies, drained, optional

In a large skillet, brown ground beef and drain off fat. Add water and Santa Fe Skillet Casserole Mix and stir until the mixture is well blended. Cook over medium-high heat until sauce thickens. If desired, add green chilies and heat through.

Santa Fe Skillet Casserole

1 jar Santa Fe Skillet
  Casserole Mix
1 lb. ground beef

2 C. water
1 (4.5 oz.) can chopped green
  chilies, drained, optional

In a large skillet, brown ground beef and drain off fat. Add water and Santa Fe Skillet Casserole Mix and stir until the mixture is well blended. Cook over medium-high heat until sauce thickens. If desired, add green chilies and heat through.

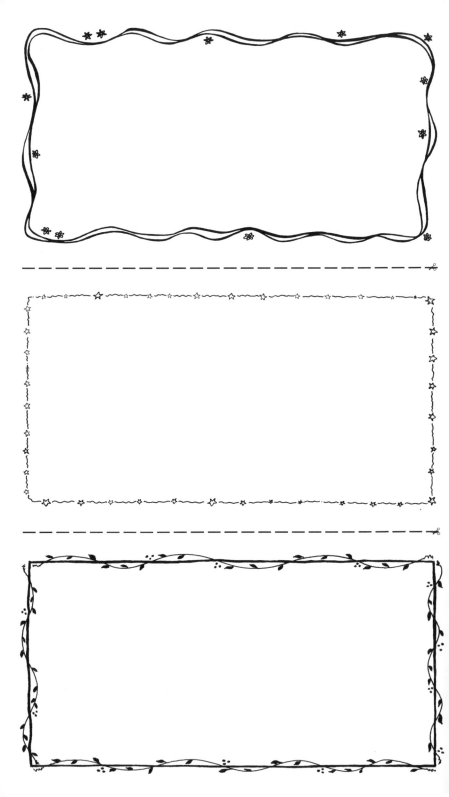

Santa Fe Skillet Casserole

1 jar Santa Fe Skillet
  Casserole Mix
1 lb. ground beef

2 C. water
1 (4.5 oz.) can chopped green
  chilies, drained, optional

In a large skillet, brown ground beef and drain off fat. Add water and Santa Fe Skillet Casserole Mix and stir until the mixture is well blended. Cook over medium-high heat until sauce thickens. If desired, add green chilies and heat through.

Santa Fe Skillet Casserole

1 jar Santa Fe Skillet
  Casserole Mix
1 lb. ground beef

2 C. water
1 (4.5 oz.) can chopped green
  chilies, drained, optional

In a large skillet, brown ground beef and drain off fat. Add water and Santa Fe Skillet Casserole Mix and stir until the mixture is well blended. Cook over medium-high heat until sauce thickens. If desired, add green chilies and heat through.

Santa Fe Skillet Casserole

1 jar Santa Fe Skillet
  Casserole Mix
1 lb. ground beef

2 C. water
1 (4.5 oz.) can chopped green
  chilies, drained, optional

In a large skillet, brown ground beef and drain off fat. Add water and Santa Fe Skillet Casserole Mix and stir until the mixture is well blended. Cook over medium-high heat until sauce thickens. If desired, add green chilies and heat through.

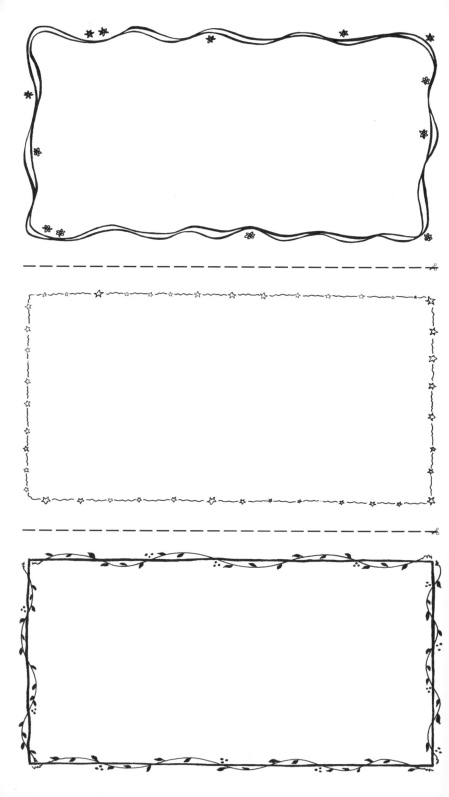

Tuna & Noodle Casserole Mix

3/4 C. Parmesan cheese
1 (1.4 oz.) pkg. Knorr Vegetable
  Soup mix
1/2 C. instant dry milk
2 1/2 C. egg noodles

Layer the ingredients in the order given into a wide-mouth 1-quart canning jar. Pack each layer in place before adding the next ingredient.

Attach a gift tag with the cooking directions.

❀ *Gifts in a jar make great bake sale items* ❀

Tuna & Noodle Casserole

1 jar Tuna & Noodle Casserole
   Mix
2 1/2 C. water
1 (6 oz.) can tuna

In a medium skillet, place Tuna & Noodle Casserole Mix and water. Over medium-high heat, heat to a boil, stirring often. Reduce heat to medium and cook until noodles are tender, stirring often. Add tuna and heat through.

Tuna & Noodle Casserole

1 jar Tuna & Noodle
Casserole Mix

2 1/2 C. water
1 (6 oz.) can tuna

In a medium skillet, place Tuna & Noodle Casserole Mix and water. Over medium-high heat, heat to a boil, stirring often. Reduce heat to medium and cook until noodles are tender, stirring often. Add tuna and heat through.

Tuna & Noodle Casserole

1 jar Tuna & Noodle
Casserole Mix

2 1/2 C. water
1 (6 oz.) can tuna

In a medium skillet, place Tuna & Noodle Casserole Mix and water. Over medium-high heat, heat to a boil, stirring often. Reduce heat to medium and cook until noodles are tender, stirring often. Add tuna and heat through.

Tuna & Noodle Casserole

1 jar Tuna & Noodle
Casserole Mix

2 1/2 C. water
1 (6 oz.) can tuna

In a medium skillet, place Tuna & Noodle Casserole Mix and water. Over medium-high heat, heat to a boil, stirring often. Reduce heat to medium and cook until noodles are tender, stirring often. Add tuna and heat through.

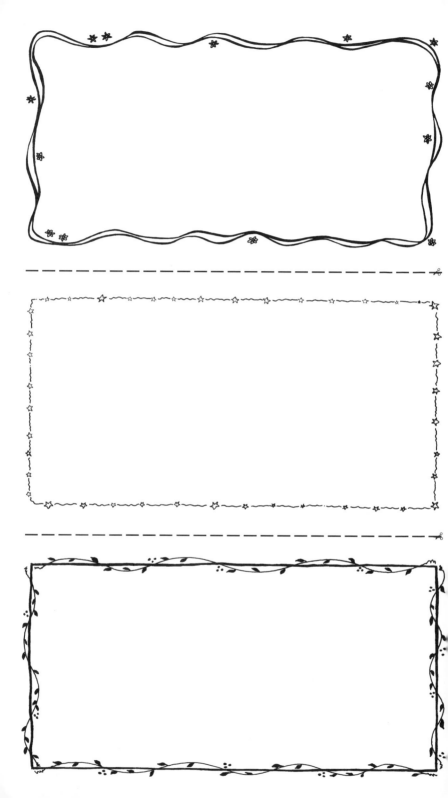

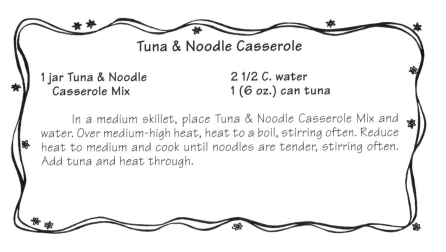

Tuna & Noodle Casserole

1 jar Tuna & Noodle
  Casserole Mix

2 1/2 C. water
1 (6 oz.) can tuna

    In a medium skillet, place Tuna & Noodle Casserole Mix and water. Over medium-high heat, heat to a boil, stirring often. Reduce heat to medium and cook until noodles are tender, stirring often. Add tuna and heat through.

Tuna & Noodle Casserole

1 jar Tuna & Noodle
  Casserole Mix

2 1/2 C. water
1 (6 oz.) can tuna

    In a medium skillet, place Tuna & Noodle Casserole Mix and water. Over medium-high heat, heat to a boil, stirring often. Reduce heat to medium and cook until noodles are tender, stirring often. Add tuna and heat through.

Tuna & Noodle Casserole

1 jar Tuna & Noodle
  Casserole Mix

2 1/2 C. water
1 (6 oz.) can tuna

    In a medium skillet, place Tuna & Noodle Casserole Mix and water. Over medium-high heat, heat to a boil, stirring often. Reduce heat to medium and cook until noodles are tender, stirring often. Add tuna and heat through.

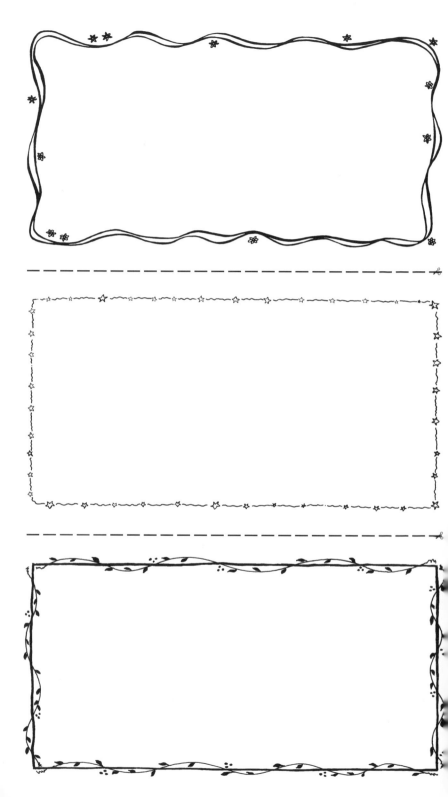

Goulash Mix

1/2 C. dried minced onion
1 1/2 tsp. salt
1 1/2 tsp. chili powder
1/2 to 3/4 tsp. pepper
3/4 tsp. sugar
3 C. elbow macaroni

Layer the ingredients in the order given into a wide-mouth 1-quart canning jar. Pack each layer in place before adding the next ingredient.

Attach a gift tag with the cooking directions.

❀ *To make a gift in a jar fancier, decorate it with a doily and ribbon.* ❀

Goulash

1 jar Goulash Mix
1 1/2 lbs. ground beef
3 (14 1/2 oz.) cans stewed
   tomatoes
1 C. water

In a large skillet, brown ground beef and drain off fat. Add tomatoes and water, bring to a boil. Reduce heat and simmer for 5 minutes. Stir in Goulash Mix; cover and simmer for 15 minutes. Uncover; simmer until macaroni is tender and sauce is thickened.

Goulash

1 jar Goulash Mix
1 1/2 lbs. ground beef

3 (14 1/2 oz.) cans stewed tomatoes
1 C. water

In a large skillet, brown ground beef and drain off fat. Add tomatoes and water, bring to a boil. Reduce heat and simmer for 5 minutes. Stir in Goulash Mix; cover and simmer for 15 minutes. Uncover; simmer until macaroni is tender and sauce is thickened.

Goulash

1 jar Goulash Mix
1 1/2 lbs. ground beef

3 (14 1/2 oz.) cans stewed tomatoes
1 C. water

In a large skillet, brown ground beef and drain off fat. Add tomatoes and water, bring to a boil. Reduce heat and simmer for 5 minutes. Stir in Goulash Mix; cover and simmer for 15 minutes. Uncover; simmer until macaroni is tender and sauce is thickened.

Goulash

1 jar Goulash Mix
1 1/2 lbs. ground beef

3 (14 1/2 oz.) cans stewed tomatoes
1 C. water

In a large skillet, brown ground beef and drain off fat. Add tomatoes and water, bring to a boil. Reduce heat and simmer for 5 minutes. Stir in Goulash Mix; cover and simmer for 15 minutes. Uncover; simmer until macaroni is tender and sauce is thickened.

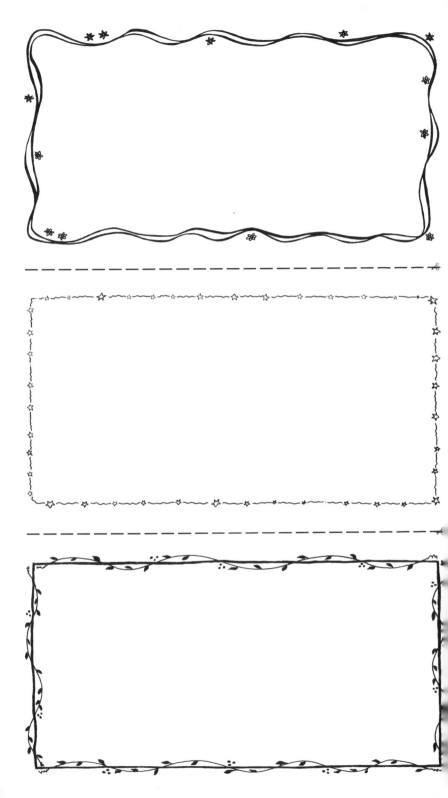

Turkey Bow Tie Skillet Mix

2 T. dried celery flakes
3 T. dried minced onion
1/4 tsp. dried minced garlic
1 T. chicken bouillon granules
1 tsp. sugar
3/4 tsp. chili powder
3/4 tsp. garlic salt
3 C. bow tie pasta

Topping Packet:
3 T. Parmesan cheese
1 tsp. dried parsley flakes

Layer the ingredients in the order given into a wide-mouth 1-quart canning jar. Pack each layer in place before adding the next ingredient. Mix and place the toppings in a small plastic bag. Place the packet on top of the pasta.

Attach a gift tag with the cooking directions.

Turkey Bow Tie Skillet

1 jar Turkey Bow Tie Skillet Mix
1 lb. ground turkey
1 T. vegetable oil
3 C. water
1 (14 1/2 oz.) can stewed
   tomatoes

In a large skillet, brown turkey in oil. Remove turkey and keep warm. Add water to pan, bring to a boil. Remove baggie from jar and add the rest of the Turkey Bow Tie Skillet Mix to the skillet. Cook for 10 minutes or until pasta is tender. Reduce heat and stir in tomatoes and turkey mixture. Simmer for 10 minutes or until heated through. Sprinkle with baggie contents and stir.

Turkey Bow Tie Skillet

1 jar Turkey Bow Tie Skillet Mix
1 lb. ground turkey
1 T. vegetable oil

3 C. water
1 (14 1/2 oz.) can stewed
   tomatoes

In a large skillet, brown turkey in oil. Remove turkey and keep warm. Add water to pan, bring to a boil. Remove baggie from jar and add the rest of the Turkey Bow Tie Skillet Mix to the skillet. Cook for 10 minutes or until pasta is tender. Reduce heat and stir in tomatoes and turkey mixture. Simmer for 10 minutes or until heated through. Sprinkle with baggie contents and stir.

Turkey Bow Tie Skillet

1 jar Turkey Bow Tie Skillet Mix
1 lb. ground turkey
1 T. vegetable oil

3 C. water
1 (14 1/2 oz.) can stewed
   tomatoes

In a large skillet, brown turkey in oil. Remove turkey and keep warm. Add water to pan, bring to a boil. Remove baggie from jar and add the rest of the Turkey Bow Tie Skillet Mix to the skillet. Cook for 10 minutes or until pasta is tender. Reduce heat and stir in tomatoes and turkey mixture. Simmer for 10 minutes or until heated through. Sprinkle with baggie contents and stir.

Turkey Bow Tie Skillet

1 jar Turkey Bow Tie Skillet Mix
1 lb. ground turkey
1 T. vegetable oil

3 C. water
1 (14 1/2 oz.) can stewed
   tomatoes

In a large skillet, brown turkey in oil. Remove turkey and keep warm. Add water to pan, bring to a boil. Remove baggie from jar and add the rest of the Turkey Bow Tie Skillet Mix to the skillet. Cook for 10 minutes or until pasta is tender. Reduce heat and stir in tomatoes and turkey mixture. Simmer for 10 minutes or until heated through. Sprinkle with baggie contents and stir.

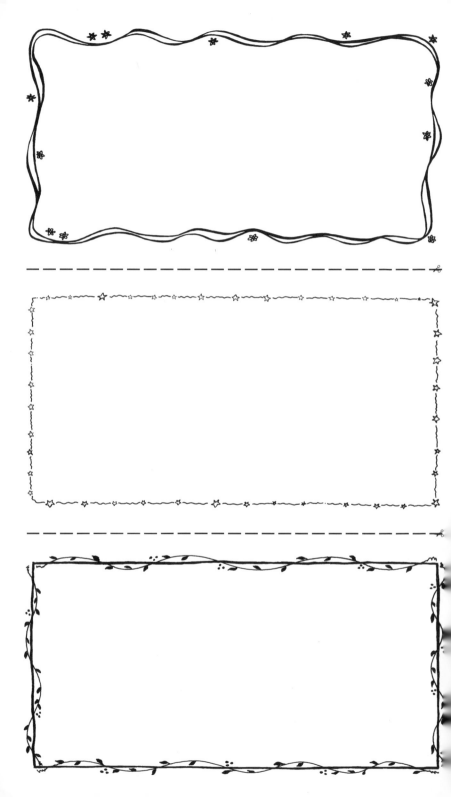

Turkey Bow Tie Skillet

1 jar Turkey Bow Tie Skillet Mix
1 lb. ground turkey
1 T. vegetable oil

3 C. water
1 (14 1/2 oz.) can stewed
   tomatoes

    In a large skillet, brown turkey in oil. Remove turkey and keep warm. Add water to pan, bring to a boil. Remove baggie from jar and add the rest of the Turkey Bow Tie Skillet Mix to the skillet. Cook for 10 minutes or until pasta is tender. Reduce heat and stir in tomatoes and turkey mixture. Simmer for 10 minutes or until heated through. Sprinkle with baggie contents and stir.

Turkey Bow Tie Skillet

1 jar Turkey Bow Tie Skillet Mix
1 lb. ground turkey
1 T. vegetable oil

3 C. water
1 (14 1/2 oz.) can stewed
   tomatoes

    In a large skillet, brown turkey in oil. Remove turkey and keep warm. Add water to pan, bring to a boil. Remove baggie from jar and add the rest of the Turkey Bow Tie Skillet Mix to the skillet. Cook for 10 minutes or until pasta is tender. Reduce heat and stir in tomatoes and turkey mixture. Simmer for 10 minutes or until heated through. Sprinkle with baggie contents and stir.

Turkey Bow Tie Skillet

1 jar Turkey Bow Tie Skillet Mix
1 lb. ground turkey
1 T. vegetable oil

3 C. water
1 (14 1/2 oz.) can stewed
   tomatoes

    In a large skillet, brown turkey in oil. Remove turkey and keep warm. Add water to pan, bring to a boil. Remove baggie from jar and add the rest of the Turkey Bow Tie Skillet Mix to the skillet. Cook for 10 minutes or until pasta is tender. Reduce heat and stir in tomatoes and turkey mixture. Simmer for 10 minutes or until heated through. Sprinkle with baggie contents and stir.

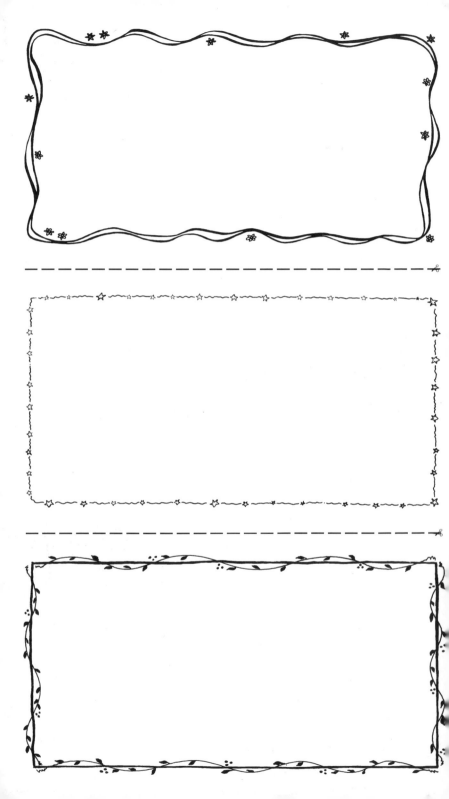